ASTRONOMY FOR THE AMATEUR

JOHN GRIBBIN

David McKay Company, Inc.
New York

Title page: The Orion Nebula

c/ Jun 80 2.78 19765

Acknowledgments

The publishers are grateful to the following for supply illustrations:

Michael Batchelor: 14; Fullerscopes: 31, 35, 53, 66, 68, 70;
Bob Halliday: 12; David Hughes: 23; Brian Jobson: 79;
Lick Observatory: title page, 13, 29, 36–7, 42–3, 63, 74, 75;
Nature: 86; Robert McNaught: 46–7, 58–9; Chris Mitchell: 10, 80;
Clive Nanson: 81; NASA: 64; NCAR: 49; Pergamon Press Ltd.: 51, 52;
Royal Astronomical Society: 17, 18, 24–5, 41, 44, 48, 50, 54 (Hale
Observatories), 56. 57, 62 (Hale Observatories), 67 (Hale
Observatories), 69, 71, 73; Royal Greenwich Observatory: 45;
Robin Scagell: 55; Science Research Council: 39; D. Strange: 28;
J. Thomas: 15, 16.
Line drawings by Sally Godwin

Library of Congress Cataloging in Publication Data
Gribbin, John R
   Astronomy for the amateur.
   Bibliography: p.
   Includes index.
   1. Astronomy – Popular works. I. Title.
QB44.2.G75   520   76-27607
ISBN 0-679-20384-2

Printed in Great Britain

Contents

Introduction: Why Astronomy?

A lot of people today talk about the 'swing away from science', but I see this more as a swing of science, as presented by scientists, away from the interests of ordinary people. Too much of science has lost the original sense of wonder which can make the study of the world about us so exciting. But one science which seems unlikely ever to lose this sense of wonder is astronomy. One of the hidden blessings of a powercut in the cold of January is that it enables city dwellers to notice those remarkable lights in the sky, the stars.

Astronomy certainly brings out our sense of wonder and curiosity—and once that curiosity is aroused, we can look into the science further with no more equipment than our own eyes, aided by binoculars or a telescope if one is wanted. Of course, you can spend as much as you want on aids to view the heavens—but you need not spend anything at all (except time!) to have a fascinating and rewarding hobby. This book is intended for those who have noticed the fascinating lights in the sky and would like to know a little more about them. I cannot provide very many answers in such a short space, but I hope to provide a few hints, and a guide to where more answers can be found and where others with similar interests can be contacted, that will prove useful to anyone who, unlike many 'scientists', still retains that sense of wonder.

1 Lights in the Sky

Now that so many people live in brightly lit—and sometimes smogbound—cities few of us realize just how spectacular the night sky can be on a clear and moonless night. The story is told that during the early weeks of 1973, when power restrictions in London caused by a shortage of coal had led to the imposition of something like a total blackout, police stations were inundated with reports of strange lights in the sky. Usually, the callers attributed these lights to supernatural phenomena or unidentified flying objects; in every case, it turned out that all they were seeing were the natural lights in the sky—stars, planets and meteors. The story may be apocryphal. But the fact that it is told at all reveals how far removed we are from our not so distant ancestors, to whom the changing patterns of the night sky must have been an integral part of life.

So, before moving on to the practicalities of investigating those lights in the sky, and providing some guidance for those who wish to make astronomy a serious hobby, it seems best to start from the very beginning, and explain those lights as if to someone who had never noticed them before. Some readers may find this too basic a beginning; if you are one of them, by all means move on to the next chapter at once. But for the rest—and that will include most city dwellers—new astronomers begin here.

Stars

Most of the lights in the sky are stars. Our own Sun is a star, and a rather ordinary star at that; the only reason that it seems so bright and impressive is that it is so very much closer to us than all the other stars in the sky.

In the nature of things, the stars are by far the most important objects visible in the sky. They are hot and bright because they generate their own energy through nuclear reactions going on deep inside them, and probably a great many stars have their own families of planets orbiting around them. Everything else that we can see in the sky with our unaided eyes belongs much closer to home, and is part of our own Sun's family of planets and cosmic junk—the Solar System. But even the faintest and most insignificant-looking star you can see could have its own Solar System, planets and all, with perhaps even its own astronomers, gazing into the sky and noticing our own Sun as a faint and rather insignificant star.

But to the amateur observer on Earth, the stars are important for another reason. Because of their great distance from us, the stars form a pattern in the sky which is almost unchanging from year to year. These distances are hard to visualize; our own Sun, which is 860,000 miles in diameter, is 93 *million* miles away from us, and yet that distance is insignificant on the cosmic scale. To get any grasp of the distances to the stars, it is best to follow the professional astronomers and measure distance by the time it takes for light to cross it.

This approach provides a measure called the **light year**—a measure of distance, not time. Light takes $8\frac{1}{2}$ minutes to travel from the Sun to the Earth, at the enormous speed of 186,000 miles a second. In other words, the distance from the Sun to the Earth is $8\frac{1}{2}$ light minutes, and if anything happens on the surface of the Sun it is $8\frac{1}{2}$ minutes before observers on Earth can see it happen. On the same sort of scale, the distance to the Moon is a mere $1\frac{1}{4}$ light seconds. Even that is noticeable these days, however, thanks to the televising of the Apollo Moon flights.

Radio waves travel at the same speed as light, so when ground control in Houston was talking to astronauts on the Moon, it took $1\frac{1}{4}$ seconds for the signals to reach them. Then, even if the astronauts replied at once it took another $1\frac{1}{4}$ seconds for their reply to get back to Earth. So there was always a delay of $2\frac{1}{2}$ seconds between question and answer. This same delay has been very important in the Soviet unmanned Moon programme. Their Lunokhod Moon vehicles were controlled by a TV and radio link from Earth, and the operators always had to remember that their instructions would take a definite time to reach the Lunokhod—and that it would then be another $1\frac{1}{4}$ seconds before the operators could see on their TV screens just how the Lunokhod was responding to the instructions.

Operating vehicles by remote control on Mars would be even more difficult, because light signals (and radio waves) take several minutes to reach the red planet. This is why the Viking spacecraft destined to land on Mars soon are entirely automatic. But even these problems pale into insignificance when we contemplate the distances to the stars.

Even the nearest star is $4\frac{1}{2}$ light years away, a distance of about 24 million million miles. Our own family of stars, the Milky Way Galaxy, is thousands of light years across. So all the stars you can see with the unaided eye are somewhere between $4\frac{1}{2}$ and a few thousand light years away.

Of course, such huge distances are impossible to relate to our everyday experience. But at least they do explain why the star patterns—the constellations—are seemingly unchanging.

A high flying aircraft will seem to move only slowly across the sky, even though it is flying at hundreds of miles an hour. A car passing nearby will seem to move much faster, even though its real speed is only a few tens of miles per hour. And this effect of distance seeming to slow down movement, when magnified over distances of light years, explains why we cannot see the movements of the stars in a human lifetime. The only real movement of the stars that we can see is not caused by their motion at all, but by the rotation of the Earth.

Because the Earth turns on its axis every 24 hours, we see the Sun apparently rise in the East, pass overhead and set in the West. The same thing happens to the stars. The ancients thought that the Earth was fixed, with the sun and stars passing overhead mounted on some great globe surrounding the Earth, and it's easy to see why they got this impression. In fact, for most purposes it does not matter which picture you choose, certainly no one today is likely to stop using the expressions 'rise' and 'set' for the Sun and stars, even though we know that it is really the Earth's motion, not the

Above: The Plough, or Big Dipper—direct photography by amateur Chris Mitchell: 15 seconds exposure at f1.4, TRI-X film

motion of the Sun and stars, which produces these effects.

The patterns of stars we can see vary according to the time of year. This change is also caused by the Earth's motion through space. By and large, however, the stars may be treated as 'fixed' for the purposes of the amateur astronomer. And since watching something that is always the same is a bit boring and futile, studies of the 'fixed' stars do not have much place in amateur astronomy.

Some stars do vary in brightness, and these can be the subject of fascinating study, as I shall describe later. But the main use of the stars for the kinds of observation described in this book is that they provide the constant background, or map, against which you can mark the changes which are occurring in the more interesting objects in the sky.

This is one reason why amateurs can still contribute worthwhile observations to the science of astronomy. Professional astronomers have the equipment to study faint objects and very subtle changes, and naturally they try to press their equipment to the limits. Thus there is a very real chance that more obvious changes in the pattern of the lights in the sky might be missed without a little help from their friends the amateurs. The professionals are well equipped to see the individual 'trees' of the stellar wood, but the amateur can quickly spot changes in the obvious features of the whole 'wood'.

In many books for amateur astronomers—or even in the pages of some newspapers—you will find fairly detailed sky maps showing the patterns of the stars, or **constellations.** There are a lot of constellations, and most of these patterns seem to have been picked out by someone with fantastic eyesight and more imagination than common sense, judging from the names given to some groups of stars. For the life of me I cannot see any way of making such constellations as Aries look anything like the creatures they are supposed to represent, and the prospect of trying to use these features as a 'map' of the sky is terrifying. How can we ever expect to locate any particular star out of the three thousand or so visible to the naked eye?

The answer is simple. Ignore most of the constellations altogether. All you really need is to be able to recognize about three of the most significant patterns in the sky. In the northern hemisphere, the Plough is the most obvious, and it even looks like a plough (it doesn't look anything like a bear, so I shall ignore its alternative name of The Great Bear!). Although the constellation Orion bears no resemblance at all to a hunter, it is very easy to pick out—the four bright stars at the corners of a large rectangle, with the three stars of Orion's Belt crossing the 'waist'. And the only other constellation I could point to is Cassiopeia, which is a nice, clear W shape on the sky.

If I lived in the southern hemisphere, I'd hope to be able to pick out the Southern Cross and a couple of other constellations, and the Magellanic Clouds more than make up for the absence of a southern 'pole star' as landmarks (as long, of course, as you don't need to find due south in a hurry!). But three good, clear patterns are all you need to find your way about the sky.

The trick is simple. If you want to find any particular object, look up its position in a reference book, and look up the position of the

Right: The large Magellanic
Cloud, photographed through
a 6" aperture telescope. Top:
The Pleiades and Hyades, in
direct photography by
amateur Bob Halliday: 20
seconds exposure at f2.8,
TRI-X rated at 1500 ASA.
Bottom: The familiar 'W' of
Cassiopeia, in direct
photography by amateur Bob
Halliday: 20 seconds
exposure at f2.8, TRI-X rated
at 1500 ASA

nearest of your three familiar friends in the sky (pretty soon you'll find you don't need to look up the position of Orion any more!). Then you can find the object you want simply by going, say, 'north a bit and a bit more to the west' of something you can already find easily.

Of course, the fainter the object you are looking for, the harder it gets. But any sensible beginner starting out with the interesting bright objects will graduate by easy stages to finding interesting faint objects almost without knowing it, and quite painlessly. The system also works in reverse. If you see something odd going on, with a bit of practice you will be able to judge fairly accurately where the interesting event is in relation to friend Orion, or the central star in Cassiopeia, and that will enable you to compare notes with other observers with confidence that you have all been looking at the same thing.

Even the pattern of the fixed stars varies with the seasons, but this is due to the movement of the Earth through space and not to movements of the stars themselves. Because the Earth is tilted, so that its axis is not quite perpendicular to a line joining the centre of the Earth with the centre of the Sun, we do not look straight out along a line joining the Sun and Earth when we look at the night sky overhead at midnight. As the Earth moves round the Sun, this line of sight shifts slightly above and below the plane of the Sun's equator, with the result that the pattern of stars shifts north and south as the seasons progress. Some constellations are visible only in the Northern Hemisphere, others only in the Southern; but a great many are seasonal, rising above the horizon from the direction of the equator only at certain times of year.

Planets and satellites

The most obvious regular wanderers among the fixed patterns of the stars are the planets. Our planet, the Earth, is about eight thousand miles in diameter, and just as the Sun is a pretty unimpressive star, so the Earth is a pretty unimpressive planet—at least in terms of size. There are nine planets altogether in our Solar System, each at a different distance from the Sun and each moving round the Sun at its own speed. The closer a planet is to the Sun, the faster it moves around. The Earth is the third planet out from the Sun, and because of the movements of all the planets, including the Earth itself, we can see them following sometimes rather odd paths across the sky. This movement of the planets clearly distinguishes them from the 'fixed' stars. Planets also differ from stars in that they do not 'twinkle', while some of them are very bright at certain times, with steady colours obvious even to the naked eye.

The range of variations is large even within the Solar System. Mercury, the closest planet to the Sun, orbits once in three months while Pluto, the most distant, takes two hundred and fifty years to get round its orbit, at a distance of more than $3\frac{1}{2}$ thousand million miles from the Sun.

Some of the planets are very easily picked out. If ever you see a bright 'star' shining all alone just after the Sun has set (or just before it rises) you are almost certainly looking at **Venus,** which appears as the evening 'star' or morning 'star' at different times during its orbit. An object which is almost as bright as Venus, but can appear at any time of the night and anywhere in the circle of sky from east through south (or north to an observer in southern latitudes) to west, is **Jupiter.** This is just about the easiest object to identify in the night sky apart from the Moon—and the next easiest is **Mars,** which really does look red and can appear quite bright when it is at its closest to the Earth.

Below: Venus and Jupiter in direct photography by amateur J. Thomas: approximately 15 seconds exposure at f2.8 FP4 rated at 200 ASA

These are all easy to spot with the unaided eye. But given even a low-powered telescope or pair of binoculars, a look at Jupiter reveals a striking new sight—the planet itself is accompanied by four moons, or satellites, which appear as bright dots strung out like beads on a wire near Jupiter.

These Jovian satellites have great historic importance, and their discovery was a key factor in persuading astronomers that just as these moons circle Jupiter, so Jupiter and all the planets orbit the Sun. Other planets too have satellites. Jupiter has a whole family of a dozen or so (new ones are still being detected, so the exact number may be out of date by the time you read this), but you'll be lucky to see more than four without a decent telescope. Saturn not only has a family of satellites, but also a spectacular ring system well worth seeing through a telescope. But the Earth has its own special kind of satellites—in addition to one large natural Moon, there are now scores of artificial satellites in orbit around our planet, and many of them are easily visible, as they reflect the Sun's light.

Comets and meteors

The Sun has a second family of dependants, which together with the planets and their satellites, make up the Solar System. These are the comets. Comets behave more extravagantly than planets. Instead of always keeping much the same distance from the Sun, as planets do, comets sweep around in very tight, elliptical orbits. The orbits are so long and narrow that for most of the time a comet is out beyond Pluto, only dashing in for a close sweep past the Sun at rare intervals.

18

Comets are also much more ephemeral than planets, being
made up of frozen gases, ice and dust in a loose cloud with only a
small compact 'head' or nucleus. It is only when a comet comes
near the Sun that it gets hot enough for this ice to evaporate, producing a glowing tail which can be quite spectacular. In fact, we
are well overdue for a good bright comet, on the law of averages,
but even a more ordinary comet can be a fine sight through a
telescope.

As comets orbit the Sun, they lose some of the bits and pieces of
dust they contain, and this minute cosmic debris often reaches the
Earth, wandering in its own orbit around the Sun. When that
happens, each dust grain glows briefly but brightly as it burns up in
the Earth's atmosphere, and is called a meteor. Very rarely, a large
chunk of rock actually reaches the ground, perhaps blasting out a
great crater. Then, it is called a meteorite.

This really brings us back to where we began this chapter. On a
clear, dark night in the country you can expect to see ten or more
meteors in an hour, and a lot more at certain times of the year. But
a city dweller might never see one—unless there is a power cut!
And a glowing fireball streaking across the sky can be very surprising to the uninitiated, even to someone who might laugh at the
thought that the sight of the stars could be a novelty.

But now we are initiated into the mysteries of those lights in the
sky. We're not going to phone the police to report a meteor as
being a flying saucer. So what can we actually learn from looking at
these lights in the sky—and what can amateurs actually contribute
to the scientific study of the heavens?

2 Naked Eye Observations

Astronomy must be almost unique among hobbies in that you can get something worthwhile out of it without using any equipment at all. This is because nature provides us with one of the most remarkable observing instruments available—the human eye, which, for many purposes, cannot be bettered by any artificial equipment.

Telescopes can see fainter objects than the eye can, and they can 'see' at different parts of the spectrum. But there is nothing to beat the combination of human eye and human brain for taking a general look at the whole sky and noticing anything odd that is going on.

It is possible (but not very likely) that you might discover a **nova** – the bright flaring up of a faint star to appear as a 'new' star to the naked eye. Novas are not too common, and you could only expect to find one if you had such a thorough knowledge of the patterns of the constellations that you could recognize an extra star as something that did not belong in the pattern. You certainly won't *discover* a comet without the aid of a telescope—too many people are already using telescopes and cameras to search for comets. But they can be well worth watching with even the simplest observing equipment (ordinary binoculars hardly count as specialist equipment, but they can transform the casual activity of sky watching). And incidentally, if you ever do discover a comet, then the scientific convention is that it will be named after you—that's one reason why so many people are on the lookout for them.

There are, however, two kinds of astronomical objects for which naked eye observations are really the only ones worth making. These are artificial satellites and visual meteors. In fact, some kinds of meteors are also studied by radio astronomers using a radar echo technique—but no one tries to study them with optical telescopes.

Artificial satellites

Since 4 October 1957 a bewildering variety of man-made probes have been launched into space. When the first sputniks appeared in the sky, some of the older, establishment astronomers were heard to mutter darkly into their beards about this irresponsible 'pollution' of the skies, ruining their chances of making decent observations! Things are not really quite that bad, even today, but these artificial moons do pose some problems.

Orbits of satellites cannot be forecast with complete accuracy, because even though there is very little air up where these artificial moons travel (beyond an altitude of about 150 miles), the traces of atmosphere that they do encounter provide a drag which slows them down and changes their orbits all the time. Indeed, studies of how the orbits of satellites 'decay' in this way are helping to provide a better understanding of just what the upper parts of the Earth's atmosphere are like.

Professional astronomers do track satellites by radio and radar techniques, but there are too many satellites to watch all the time, and observations from amateurs can still be very useful—provided that the observations are accurate. Actually contributing to science in this way is something to think about only after you have decided you want to make a serious hobby out of astronomy, and after you have got into contact with local and national societies through which contributions of this kind can be channelled. You would certainly need to go further than the first steps outlined in this book. But it is worth knowing at the outset that you can, if you want to, make something more of this hobby than just an excuse to sit out in the cold gazing at the sky.

Anyway, even for the casual observer artificial satellites are very easy to detect. All you have to do is find something that looks like a point of light and moves steadily across the background of the stars (but remember that flashing red and green lights are attached to aeroplanes!).

Finding the brightest of these man-made moons is made even easier by some newspapers, which print details of satellites that are expected to be visible. Indeed, the whole game is so easy that it provides one way of checking up on whether you are really cut out to take astronomy seriously and start spending money on your new hobby. If you cannot find any satellites and find the whole exercise rather tiresome, you might as well give up at once and go back to doing jigsaw puzzles in the warmth and comfort of your own home.

But if you can find satellites, and would like to go one step further by making records of the observations (either for your own amusement or, perhaps, as a contribution to some organized satellite watch) then that step is almost equally simple. For this kind of work, you do really need to know a few more star patterns than the three basic 'friends' that I have mentioned before—but, of course, you can check these from standard sky atlases, so you don't actually need a photographic memory. The simplest way to 'fix' a satellite is to note the exact time at which it reaches its closest position on the sky to an identified bright star, or even better the time at which it passes between two bright stars.

To get the time accurately, it is best to work backwards, using a stopwatch. The trick is to *start* the watch at the time the satellite reaches the point you are interested in, then to check the exact time soon afterwards from a trustworthy radio time signal (not the rough and ready guide provided by most disc jockeys) or simply by using the telephone time service. Stop the watch when you get the time signal, subtract its reading from the time you have just found, and there you are—the time when the satellite reached the position you were watching.

That's about all you can do with observations of satellites. As far as the amateur astronomer is concerned, they are hardly the greatest thing since sliced bread. But on the other hand you can generate an aura of impressive expertise among your friends by pointing to an insignificant light in the sky on a starry night, checking your wristwatch, and saying 'Ah, there goes Skylab, just about on time'. But be sure you get it right—if your friends are like mine the chances are they'll check in the papers to see if that satellite really was visible when you said it was.

Meteors

With meteors, however, the naked-eye observer really comes into his own. You can see meteors on any clear night (if you don't live in a town), but they do tend to occur in 'showers' at certain times of the year. This is because the tiny particles which produce these shooting stars are associated with comets, and follow cometary orbits around the Sun. This produces a band of fine dust stretching around the entire orbit, and when the Earth ploughs through these bands of dust we get impressive meteor displays.

The particles which produce the visible trails really are tiny—a bright meteor would be made by a dust grain one tenth of an inch across, while something the size of a pea counts as a veritable giant. The spectacular display arises because of the heat generated when even tiny particles burn up in the Earth's atmosphere; and that this heat is basically coming from the kinetic energy corresponding to the speed with which the particle collides with the Earth's atmosphere.

Because the Earth itself is moving around the Sun, the speed of the 'collision' depends on whether a meteor particle hits the Earth head on, or creeps up from behind. It's pretty easy to see that we are at the 'front' of the Earth at dawn, and the 'back', as far as its motion around the Sun is concerned, at sunset. So you get better displays of meteors at dawn.

When you do see a shower of meteors, at dawn or any other time, you will find that they seem to be arriving from one point in the sky. In reality, they are all moving on parallel tracks, but this 'perspective' effect has its uses. The principal meteor showers are named after the constellations in which they appear to originate, and they will turn up in the same place year after year. One shower, for instance, which looks from the perspective as if it comes from a point in the constellation Perseus, is called the Perseids. This shower comes in August each year—but a word of caution: you won't actually see the shower, of course, unless the Earth reaches the dust stream during night in your part of the world. For many streams, it takes the Earth a couple of days to pass through the main flow of meteors, so provided the night is clear you have a good chance of a view from any part of the globe. But some streams are much narrower, producing sharper showers—the Quadrantids are the best example. It only takes a few hours for our planet to pass right through such a stream, and it's quite possible, for example, to miss it entirely in Europe only to hear galling stories of how spectacular the display was in North America just 12 hours later.

With meteors, which occur in great numbers when they are expected, and cannot be predicted at all when they are not expected, observations from as many people as possible around the world are of the greatest value to astronomy. You can find information about who to give the observations to at the end of this book; and you do really need to collaborate in order to do anything worthwhile. But it's fairly straightforward to make the actual observations.

Astronomers need to know three things about meteors: speed, height and the orbit in which they were moving. To find these, you must measure three things: the point at which the meteor trail

Right: A meteor shower
showing the radiant effect

appears, the point at which it disappears, and how long it lasts. It sounds pretty simple, but if you are doing this with the naked eye you will eventually need to know the constellations pretty well. But once again, you can start out spotting meteors for yourself and plotting them as best you can straight away. The necessary familiarity with the sky can only come with practice, so it's best to start as soon as possible.

Once you can trust your own observations, the time has come to combine them with those of other people made at the same time but from several miles away (at least). With two or more widely spaced observers, details about the meteor can easily be worked out.

Even simply counting the number of meteors visible over a certain time can still be useful for researchers—but this is really something to do the easy way nowadays, by taking a time-exposure photograph of the sky. Indeed, you can go the whole way and get a measure of the speed of a meteor from photographs, as I shall explain in Chapter 6. By joining up with other people in a fireball patrol you can make a big contribution to the study of these objects, the most insignificant members of the Solar System. But you must be the kind of person who likes the excuse to spend night after night out in the cold watching the skies. Most people—even most astronomers—find this particular study too boring and cold to contemplate. I certainly do—but that makes me even more ap-

Below: Aurora Australis photographed from a Japanese antarctic station

preciative of the efforts of those people who do go to the trouble of obtaining the invaluable records of meteor activity.

Northern and Southern Lights
In a way, it's cheating to include the **aurorae,** to give them their proper name, in this book. They are certainly lights in the sky, but they originate from inside the atmosphere and are to a large extent part of the Earth itself. But then, the Earth is a planet, and so of interest to astronomers, and the aurorae are produced by an interaction between our planet and the Sun, which surely makes them relevant even for astronomers who are not interested in the Earth.

The Northern Lights (Aurora Borealis) and Southern Lights (Aurora Australis) are only visible at their respective high latitudes. This is because they are produced by an interaction of charged particles from the Sun with the Earth's magnetic field. The magnetic field channels these charged particles down towards the poles, where, when they bombard the upper atmosphere, they make the atoms of the air glow. This glow is produced in exactly the same way as the glow in neon or other discharge tubes used in coloured lighting displays.

Because the effect is related to the Earth's magnetism, the best place to see the aurora in the northern hemisphere is from Iceland, near the magnetic pole, and not from the geographic pole. For latitudes as far south as London and New York, good displays are

pretty rare. But you may see spectacular aurorae even that far south, and especially at the time of maximum solar activity.

The Sun is not exactly a steady, unvarying star. For reasons which are still far from clear, it varies in many ways over a cycle which is, on average, about 11 years long. At the maximum of this cycle, there are many dark spots (sunspots) occurring on the Sun, together with violent bursts of activity called flares. This activity produces great bursts of charged particles which stream outwards across the Solar System, and these in turn lead to bright and frequent auroral displays on Earth.

The interaction of these particles with the Earth's magnetic field also affects radio communications, disrupts the navigation of migrating birds and homing pigeons, and affects the weather. But that is really another story.

At the end of 1975, we are almost exactly at a minimum in the cycle of solar activity. The next maximum is not due until at least 1979 (some astronomers think that peak activity will not be reached until 1982) and there really is very little chance of seeing anything much in the way of aurorae in the immediate future, unless you live well north of London or New York. If you are in such a fortunate position, however, you can do no more than just admire the pretty lights.

Once again, telescopes and binoculars are a complete waste of time, since auroral displays cover wide areas of sky. In this case, even photography is not much good, because of the speed with which the patterns of these curtains of light can change. If you look for an aurora and do not see one, it is still worth making a note of the fact, since it is only by knowing for sure on which nights there were no aurorae that the professionals can get reliable records of the frequency of these displays.

But if you do see something, you need to do a little more than just record the fact of the display. Give the position of the aurora in degrees, following the convention that due north is zero, east is 90°, south is 180° and west is 270°. In addition, make a note of the time and the shape and extent of the aurora. That done, you can settle down to enjoy the free show with a clear conscience.

There is also another light in the sky, the **Zodiacal Light** or 'false dawn', a faint cone of light produced by reflected sunlight from tiny particles spread out in the plane of the Solar System. This is more genuinely astronomical than aurorae, but it is so faint that it is masked even by moonlight and thoroughly obscured by artificial lighting near would-be observers. Unlike aurorae, the Zodiacal Light is best seen from the tropics; so unless you are really dedicated (or live deep in the country and are lucky too), there is very little chance that you will be able to do any worthwhile observing of the Zodiacal Light.

We have come to the limit of naked-eye observation. To make worthwhile observations of anything further than the phenomena mentioned in this chapter, you will need the aid of some kind of instrument.

3 Improving on Nature

You don't need a telescope to think profound thoughts about the Universe, and more than 1,500 years ago Chinese astronomers were familiar with such concepts as an infinite empty space in which the stars floated. The great Chinese astronomers also had ideas which are today remarkably reminiscent of those of relativity theory, with speculations about the nature of space, time and motion appearing in documents dated as 300 BC—2,200 years before Einstein. Although the invention of the telescope some three and a half centuries ago is commonly given the credit for breaking down the old Western ideas about 'crystal spheres' surrounding the Earth, it is intriguing that the end of the sixteenth century was also the time when these Chinese ideas began to filter out to Europe.

The Jesuits who visited China at that time did not hail the Chinese astronomical ideas as a revelation. After all, the idea of the Earth at the centre of the Universe, with stars moving around it fixed to the crystal spheres, was part of their religious dogma. Instead, they held up the Chinese ideas to ridicule, a demonstration of how backward the people were. The Jesuit Matteo Ricci, in letters written from China in 1595, said of Chinese astronomers: 'They say that there is only one sky and not ten skies; that it is empty and not solid. The stars are supposed to move in the void, instead of being attached to the firmament. . . . Where we say there is air between the spheres, they affirm there is a void.'

These ideas, held up by Ricci as 'absurdities', met with a different response among some Western thinkers. Ironically, just at the time when Western astronomy began to develop as a science, rather than a branch of religion, the Jesuits imposed orthodox religious views as a barrier to further development of Chinese astronomy, and censored news of the work of people like Copernicus. And even more ironically, it has taken the West something like 300 years to catch up, in philosophical terms, with some of the ideas of ancient Chinese astronomers.

So what really happened to astronomy in the 1600s was not just the invention of the telescope. People were ready for new ideas, and even without the telescope the support for the crystal sphere view of the heavens was pretty shaky. But when it comes to testing the detail of the philosophical ideas, then you do need something more in the way of astronomical equipment than the eyes provided by nature. The great renaissance of Western astronomy came about because the new information provided by the telescope was available to a great generation of thinkers. We may not all be Newtons, but today it is easy for each of us to have better observing equipment than any Newton had. Whether we want to go on to professional astronomical work, probing the mysteries of the Universe and testing some of the ideas which can be traced back even to those great Chinese thinkers, or whether we want to look at planets and stars as a hobby, the first steps at least are both straightforward and inexpensive.

Left: The Andromeda galaxy photographed by an amateur using a camera with 135mm lens, 5 minutes exposure at f2.8, Plus-X film

Getting a telescope

In these inflationary days, there is little point in quoting actual prices for telescopes and other equipment. But in barter terms, as a rough guide, you should be able to get something worthwhile for about the price of a couple of dozen LP records. That is not a lot of money—but it's enough to make it important that you should be quite sure that you really want a telescope before buying one. A lot of people do seem to end up with a very decorative piece of equipment that is hardly ever used for anything.

The reasons for this are, with hindsight, fairly obvious. The first few times you look through a telescope can be a revelation. Even our nearest neighbour the Moon is, at first, something worth just looking at without any thought of mapping, or searching for special features, or doing anything which might loosely be regarded as astronomical work! The Andromeda Nebula, which is a whole galaxy of stars like our own Galaxy, as are the smaller but closer Magellanic Clouds visible in the southern hemisphere, the Orion Nebula, which is a cloud of glowing gas and dust surrounding half a dozen stars within our own Galaxy, and the rings of Saturn are all spectacularly beautiful even when seen through a fairly modest telescope. But would you want to look at them every night?

Right: The Andromeda galaxy photographed by the Crossley reflector at Lick Observatory

Perhaps you can afford to acquire a telescope merely in order to admire the beautiful objects in the sky from time to time. But if your interest in astronomy is to be more than a passing whim, and if you are hoping to achieve something worthwhile through this hobby, then, as with everything else, there is a lot of routine involved. In other words, most of the time, even with a decent telescope, observational astronomy requires a lot of patience. And when I say a 'decent' telescope I am including everything right up to the new Anglo-Australian 150-inch in Australia, and the famous 200-inch on Mount Palomar. These great instruments, probing out to the fringes of the observable Universe, are used either to obtain very long exposure photographs or with electronic equipment hooked on to them. In either case, for most of the night the operator has little to do except sit around getting cold.

So the single most important thing about buying a telescope is to spend as much time as you can looking through someone else's instrument first. Talk to people who have done some observing, and if possible join in a real observing programme—not just a guided tour of the pretty things—yourself. Only then, if you still haven't given up astronomy and gone back to a nice comfortable indoor hobby, should you actually invest your own money.

If you are going to spend money on a telescope, you should read one of the specialist books about telescopes that are listed at the end of this book. First, however, you should consider the main factors affecting your choice.

The traditional image of a telescope is that of the master mariner, held to the eye by hand. But you would not get far as an astronomical observer if you adopted such a pose.

In the first place, that kind of telescope is a **refractor**—it contains lenses through which light passes and is focused to produce an image. Refractors were the first kind of telescopes; they can work very well, and there are large refractors still in use at such places as the Lick observatory. But **reflecting telescopes,** in which the light is focused to form an image from a mirror or mirrors, are much easier to construct, and can be made much bigger than refractors, so that the really big telescopes are all reflectors.

The second defect of the master mariner's pose is that you'd have trouble keeping anything astronomical in the field of view. A good firm mounting is absolutely essential for any instrument used in astronomy.

Many amateur astronomers began their observations using a 3-inch refractor, the smallest size worth using for astronomical work (the size—3 inches in this case—refers to the diameter of the main lens, which collects the light; in a reflector, the size is the diameter of the main parabolic mirror, and a 6-inch reflector is the smallest worth having). But this seems completely misguided to me. I just don't like refractors (which you can dismiss as personal prejudice if you like), but in practical terms any astronomer who wants to progress to a large instrument must end up with a reflector—so why not start out with one?

Another personal prejudice is that to my mind telescopes should not be regarded as portable. Certainly you can move, say, a 6-inch reflector from place to place, but what is the point? With anything

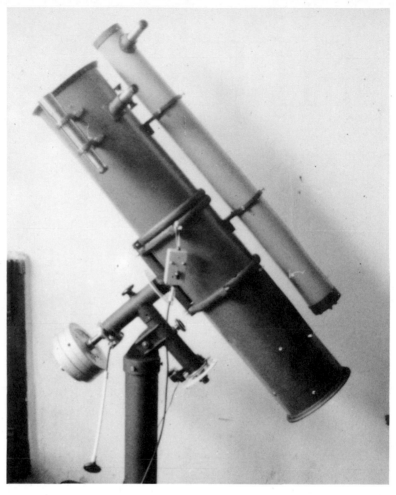

Above: A 3″ refractor.
Right: An 8″ reflector with 4″ refractor as finder

much larger than about a 10-inch reflector portability is out of the question, and besides unless you are moving a long way south or north the skies will be pretty much the same even if you do move. No, choose as good a site as possible (away from any artificial lighting, that is), forget about refractors and install a good solid reflector. With the myth of portability laid, you can happily build your own observatory, with walls to keep out the wind—but no heating, because hot air rising past the telescope will completely ruin observing conditions, or 'seeing'.

If by any chance you do for some special reason need portable equipment, for meteor or satellite watching, a good pair of binoculars is quite adequate. The only real need for moving heavy equipment is to observe an eclipse, but by the time you are ready for that you will undoubtedly be an established member of an astronomical society or club, which will be able to organize the expedition.

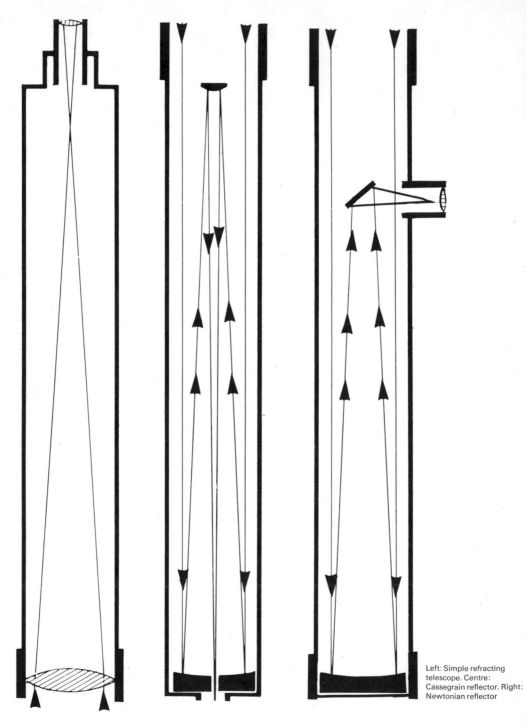

Left: Simple refracting telescope. Centre: Cassegrain reflector. Right: Newtonian reflector

With the simplest kind of reflecting telescope, the observer looks towards the mirror—in other words, away from the sky. With a plane mirror above the focusing mirror, to reflect the image, the observer may look into the telescope sideways. And with a curved mirror reflecting the light back down the telescope and through a hole in the main mirror you can even look from behind the instrument, in the 'proper' direction towards the object you are looking at!

But from whatever angle the observer views the image, he must use an **eyepiece,** which is as important to the function of the telescope as the main mirror itself. Modern eyepieces often contain quite sophisticated combinations of lenses, not unlike the lens systems used in cameras. They are designed to produce a viewable image of as much of the field of view of the telescope as possible, while keeping the image undistorted. Eyepieces can be chosen to give different magnifications of the final image, and as a general rule it is best to use the *smallest* magnification which brings into view the features you are looking for. A small, sharp picture is almost always better than a big blurred picture.

A reflector may be mounted inside a cylindrical tube, looking rather like a gun barrel, or it may simply be mounted in an openwork 'skeleton'. In either case, you will find it best to have a small refracting telescope fitted onto the tube for use as a **'finder'.** A finder is helpful because, unlike the main telescope, it has a wide field of view. If the telescopes are set up properly, all you need to do is move the instruments until the object you are interested in is at the centre of the finder's field of view, then switch to the main telescope where you should find the object nicely in the field of view.

Because of the rotation of the Earth which causes the stars to seem to drift across the sky, there might seem to be some problems in keeping the interesting object centred in the field of view for a long period of observations. But this movement is, of course, exactly regular and steady, so that it is very straightforward to have the telescope steered automatically to compensate for the rotation of the Earth. In practice, the so-called **equatorial mounting** is probably the easiest to work with. In this system, the telescope is set up so that the clock drive automatically compensates for the apparent movement of stars 'up and down' the sky, while the observer is left to follow the movement from east to west. For the really big telescopes, all the steering is done for you by a computer hooked up to the drive of the instrument. But there seems little chance of the necessary computer hardware becoming available for an amateur with a 10-inch reflector just yet.

All of this equipment, including the clock-drive and grinding of the main mirror (but not construction of the eyepiece) can be carried out by anyone who has an aptitude for 'do it yourself'. You could probably manage without any great disaster as long as you are not actually clumsy. Unfortunately, I am completely inept when it comes to such matters, and it would be quite inappropriate for me to offer any advice. So I will draw a veil over the whole ghastly business of myself and matters practical, referring those who are interested to the books cited under Further Reading.

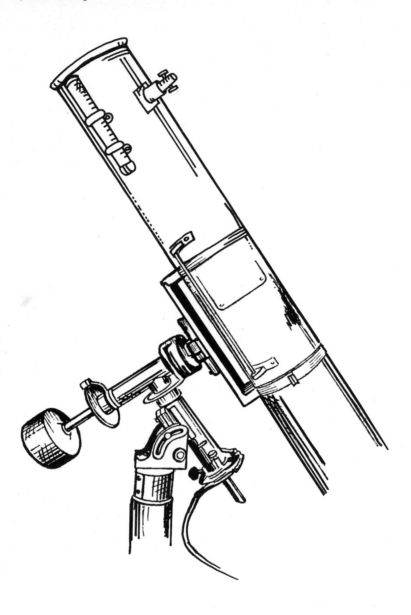

Above: An amateur's observatory

Observatories

Even a modest telescope will need some protection from the weather. A plastic cover would do, but even an incompetent such as myself can build a shed with movable roof—or better still, a shed on rails which rolls right out of the way—to make an observatory. But when it gets to the point where hundreds of thousands of pounds are invested in great reflecting telescopes, something a little more sophisticated is the order of the day.

The great observatories have several telescopes, usually sited on mountains well away from the light and dust-pollution of cities. Each big telescope has its own dome, and usually there are also offices and accommodation nearby for the use of the astronomers, who generally only visit the mountains for short periods while they are involved in observing programmes. This inaccessibility is fine for getting good observations—there are now both American and European observatories in the mountains of Chile, for example—but it makes things a bit difficult for the casual visitor who wants a look at a real observatory.

Still, in Britain, for a short time at least, there is a very large telescope which is easily accessible. The **Royal Greenwich Observatory** has been moved from Greenwich in smoky London Town to Herstmonceux in the Sussex countryside, and there the 98-inch reflector named after Isaac Newton has been operating for ten years. But even the Sussex countryside is not really a good place for such a telescope—Britain is too cloudy, and the site is almost at sea level. So in the near future the Isaac Newton Telescope is to be moved to a new site outside the UK, where a new 'Northern Hemisphere Observatory' is to be built. If you get the chance before this move takes place, visit Herstmonceux, where you can see this instrument on public view at times when visitors will not disturb the work of the observatory.

Right: A 24" reflector in an observatory used by a group of Yugoslav amateurs

35

In the USA the great telescopes are the 200-inch on **Mount Palomar** and the 120-inch at the **Lick Observatory** on Mount Hamilton, both in California. Each of these telescopes is associated with a large observatory. The story of the Lick Observatory is particularly fascinating. It seems that James Lick, who provided the finance for the building of the observatory, now rests in a tomb underneath the 36-inch refractor. He originally intended that the memorial by which the good citizens of San Francisco should remember him would be a pyramid downtown, rather larger than that of Cheops. But he was persuaded that a great observatory would be a better memorial to his name, and one was eventually built on Mount Hamilton.

Below: The Lick Observatory at Mt. Hamilton, California viewed from the east

According to Lick's bequest, the observatory should have included the biggest telescope of any in the world at that time (the late nineteenth century), but the builders cheated a little by providing the biggest *refractor* in the world. Today, pride of place on the Mountain is taken by the 120-inch reflector. This may not be the biggest in the world, but the Lick observers have long claimed that, with the aid of an impressive array of electronics, it is the best, producing a better performance even than the 200-inch on Mount Palomar. No doubt Palomar astronomers dispute this—but both now have another friendly rival which may well beat anything else now operating.

The new Anglo-Australian telescope at Siding Spring in

Australia is large, with a mirror of 150 inches diameter, and has the benefit of the experience and electronics developed over the decades that the 200-inch and 120-inch have been operating. Another reason why astronomers are so excited about the development of the Siding Spring Observatory is that there had not previously been any really large telescope in the southern hemisphere, so that half the sky remains, if not exactly uncharted, certainly not explored to any great depth.

But whether you are in the fortunate position of being one of the few astronomers allowed to use the giant reflectors, or whether your observations are restricted to those with a 6-inch reflector in the garden, there is a place for the observations in astronomy. It would be ludicrous to use the 200-inch or 120-inch to study objects in our own Solar System when they can be used to study objects so faint and remote that they would be invisible to lesser instruments. There just is not time for one telescope to look at everything. Indeed, there is so much to observe that many mysteries remain—even about the Moon, our near neighbour and the only other astronomical body to have been visited by man.

4 Observing the Sun and the Moon

The Sun and the Moon are, of course, completely different objects in astronomical terms. The Sun shines because of its own heat—nuclear reactions going on deep in the solar interior keep it hot. But the Moon is visible in the sky only because it reflects light from the Sun.

Because the Sun is so hot and, by astronomical standards, so close, we have to use special methods to observe it. It is safe to look directly at objects like the Moon through a telescope, because they only shine by reflected light. And it's safe to look directly at distant stars and galaxies through a telescope because they are so far away that very little of their light and heat reaches the Earth. But looking straight at the Sun through a telescope would cause at least serious injury, and most likely blindness.

Every book for amateur astronomers carries a warning: **do not look directly at the Sun,** yet people continue to do so. Even during an eclipse, or using a dark filter in front of the telescope, it still is not safe. So don't do it. There certainly is no need for such foolhardy behaviour, since just because the Sun is so close and hot it is very easy to observe it indirectly.

The best way to observe the Sun is by projecting the image from a telescope (plus eyepiece) on a piece of white card fixed to the telescope behind the eyepiece. The card must be shaded from the direct light of the Sun, but with a few trials it's very easy to get a good image that you can study with ease. The only extra precaution to take is that if you are lucky enough to have a fair sized telescope, stop it down to about 5 inches for a reflector or 3 inches for a refractor, or things will start to get a bit hot.

Overleaf: The Dumbell Nebula

Right: The Quiet Sun on 4 November, 1952. Below: Telescope set up for indirect viewing of sun spots

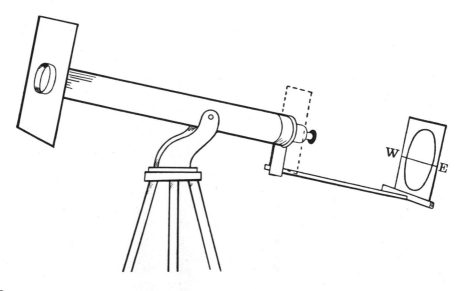

40

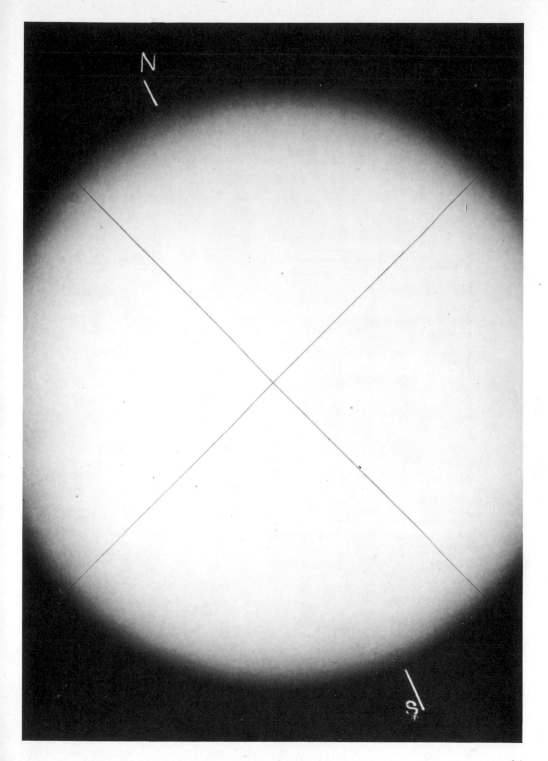

41

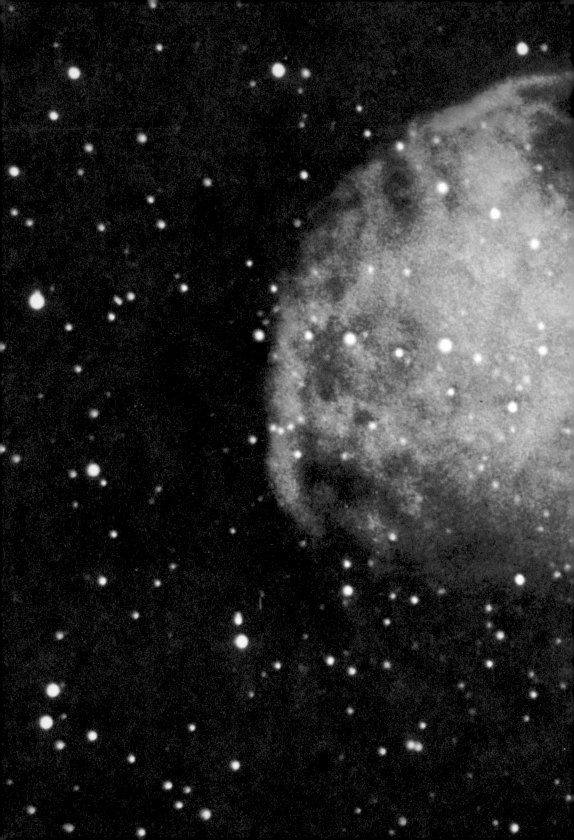

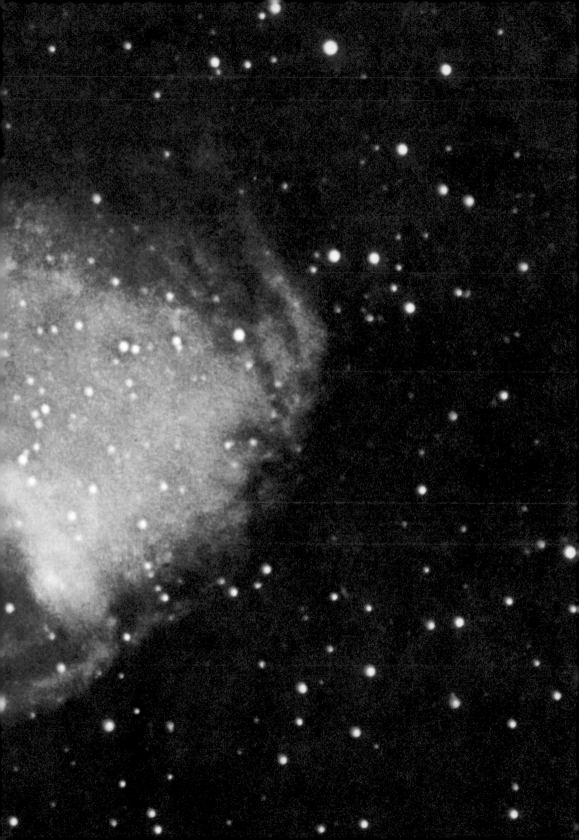

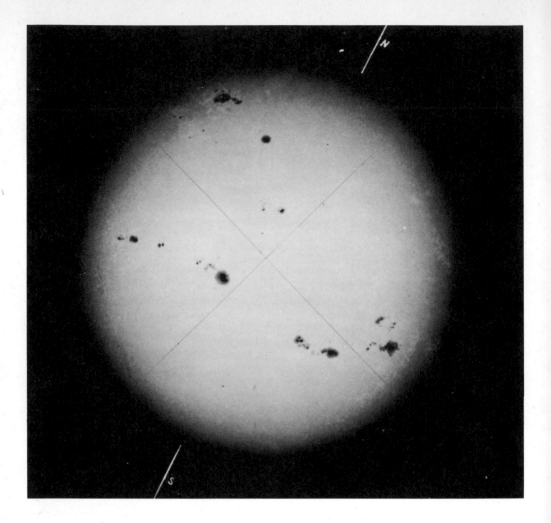

Sunspots

The most obvious feature of the Sun, when viewed in this way over a period of time, is that it is prone to spottiness. Dark spots occur in groups over the solar disc, their number and position varying from time to time. The cause of these sunspots, and the reasons for their variations, are still far from being understood, and the sections of local and national astronomical societies devoted to their study are always interested in daily records of sunspot numbers provided by other amateurs.

It's not enough just to count the number of sunspots, however, since their position is also important. It's fairly straightforward to mark up a grid pattern on a sheet of cardboard to use as the screen for projecting the Sun's image, and in this way it's easy to 'read off' the position of a spot or group of spots and mark it on a blank circle representing the Sun. If you are going to go in for this kind of study seriously, you are bound to join a local society,

Above: The sun near maximum activity on 1 April, 1958 showing heavy spotting

Overleaf: The Milky Way in Sagittarius from Hawaii, taken with a guided Nikon F camera at f1.4 with 30mm exposure

where the members have probably already got an established method of recording spots in this way. It's best to start the way you will be carrying on, so rather than give details of any particular method here I leave it to you to get in touch with other amateurs with similar interests.

Some general features of sunspots are worth mentioning in passing, so you know what you might see. The most obvious feature is that the number of sunspots varies over a fairly regular cycle, the **sunspot (or solar) cycle.** This lasts for about eleven years on average, but individual cycles can be as much as a couple of years shorter or longer.

At the beginning of a solar cycle, there are relatively few sunspots and they appear at high latitudes (about 40°) in both the northern and southern solar hemispheres. As the cycle progresses, more sunspots are seen at any one time (although individual spots and groups may last for just a couple of days or as much as 100 days), and they form closer to the solar equator. Then, after the maximum of sunspot activity for that cycle has been reached, fewer spots form in each month, but those that do form appear closer and closer to the equator, until the cycle is finished and new spots, from the next cycle, begin to appear at high latitudes. If you plot the appearance of all the spots in a series of cycles you get a pattern which is called, for obvious reasons, the 'butterfly pattern'.

Why should sunspots behave in this odd way? If you can find the answer to that one your name will certainly be remembered in the astronomical text books! Sunspots are certainly associated with changes in the magnetism of the Sun, but how and why the solar cycle takes place is very much a mystery. There is some very intriguing evidence that these changes are related to some planetary influence.

Below: The Butterfly diagram for 5 complete solar cycles, 1900–53

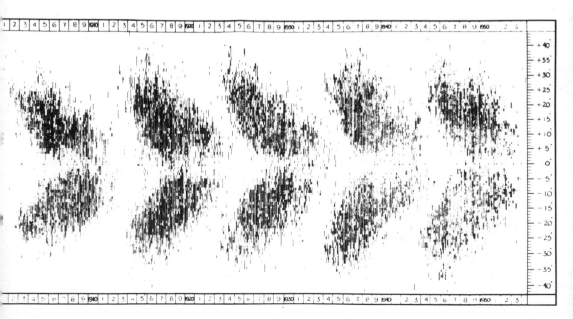

45

Because the Sun is so much more massive than everything else in the Solar System put together, the centre of mass of the whole system lies below the surface of the Sun. In the same way, incidentally, the centre of mass of the Earth-Moon system lies below the surface of the Earth. Now, as all the planets move around the Sun at their different speeds, the exact location of this Solar System centre of mass is constantly shifting within the Sun, in a stately dance.

Is it possible that it is this stirring effect which modulates the changing sunspot activity? No-one can yet say for sure, but the idea is certainly attractive, especially since calculations do suggest that the centre-of-mass motions do occur over periods very similar to those of the sunspot variations.

Whatever the cause of these changes, however, we do know one thing for sure. Observations show that 1975 was a year of minimum solar activity, with a new cycle just begun, and that the last solar maximum was at the end of 1968. It looks as if we are now experiencing a relatively long cycle, and that the next maximum will not be seen before 1980, and perhaps not till a couple of years later. For what it's worth, the theory that planets influence sunspots predicts the next maximum for 1982—so if you want to keep your own records of solar activity over the next few years you can make your own direct test of one of the most topical (and controversial) theories of present day Solar System astronomy.

Below: A sunspot group on 18 September, 1926

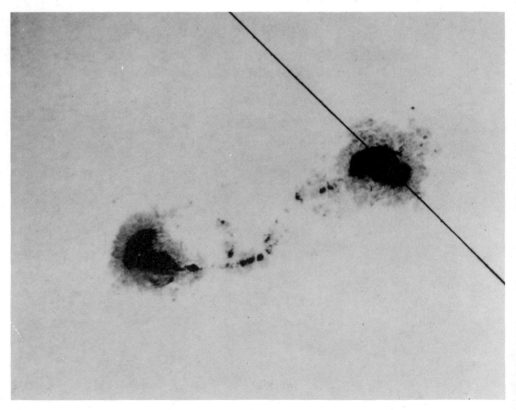

Above: A solar eclipse
showing the corona

Flares and prominences

Bright, temporary flares are occasionally seen with sunspots, but these are so rare that with a small telescope you will be lucky to see one in your lifetime. The great telescopes of the major solar observatories have shown that flares are in fact commonly associated with sunspots, but that they are usually too faint to show up on the kind of equipment an amateur is likely to possess. Indeed, unless you have more sophisticated equipment than any mentioned here, to see anything very interesting on the Sun except for the spots you really need to take advantage of a **solar eclipse.** Only a total eclipse really reveals anything out of the ordinary, and these occur so rarely, and are visible from such small areas of the Earth when they do, that I would hardly be justified in dealing with them at length here.

But to whet your appetite for the day when you may go with other members of a club or society to observe a total eclipse of the Sun, here are a few general guidelines. The most obvious revelation of a total eclipse is that the Sun extends over a far greater distance than the sharply defined disc we usually see. Great outbursts, or prominences, lick outwards from the Sun, and streamers of the glowing corona stretch still further.

Prominences are, in fact, also a feature of the variations of the solar cycle, and are often associated with sunspots. The **corona,** made of very tenuous gas, is however, a permanent feature and stretches out into space, gradually getting thinner and thinner, so that there is no real 'edge' to it. Indeed, it's quite reasonable to argue that in a very real sense our planet Earth is actually within the outer layers of the Sun's atmosphere!

When might you be able to see any of these phenomena? In Britain, not until 1999; but there will be total eclipses visible from other parts of the world well before then.

49

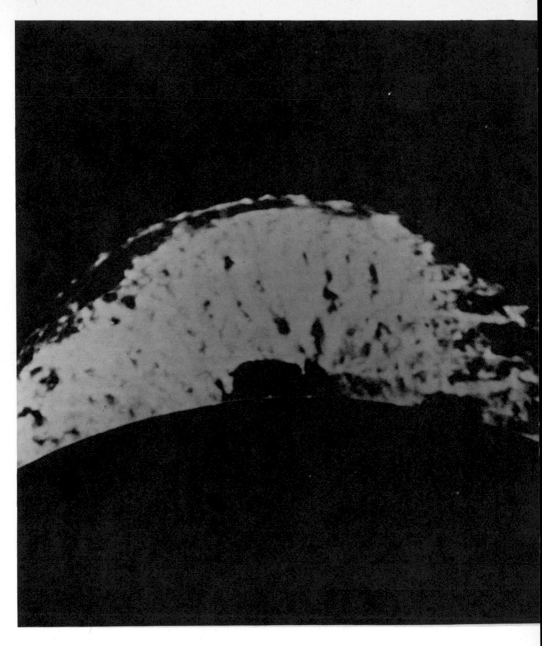

In the USA, eclipse predictions are published regularly by the US Naval Observatory in their *Circulars* (write to them at Washington DC 20390), and Number 113, published on 15 December 1966, contains details of some interesting events due shortly. On 23 October 1976 a total eclipse of the Sun will take place, and the path over which the eclipse will be visible will start in central Africa, cross the Indian Ocean and south-east Australia,

Above: A spectacular exhibition of solar activity near the maximum of a solar cycle Prominence, photographed on 4 January, 1946

ending in the Tasman Sea. The event will be visible as a partial eclipse in Australia and Tasmania.

Another total eclipse will occur on 12 October 1977, starting north-west of Hawaii, moving across the Pacific to Colombia and ending in Venezuela; this eclipse will be partial in Hawaii and all of the continental USA except the extreme north-east. But in 1979, on 26 February, Americans will have a really good total eclipse to view. This will begin in the North Pacific, cross north-western USA and central Canada and end in Greenland. The eclipse will be partial in all of North America except for the west of Alaska, in Iceland, the UK and in Brittany.

Below: Past and future eclipse paths in the Southern Hemisphere

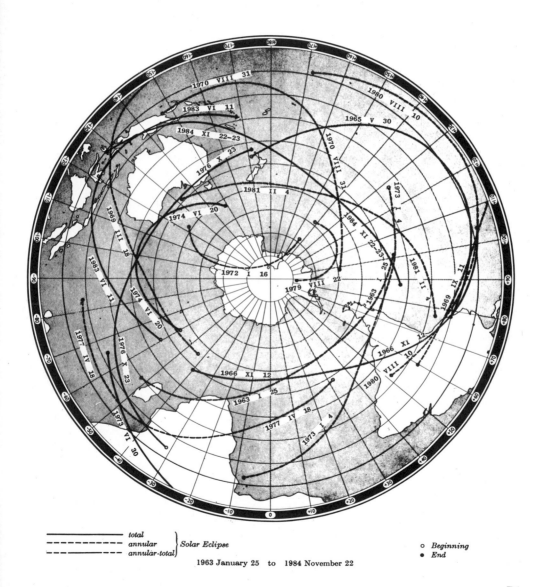

total
annular   } Solar Eclipse
annular-total

o Beginning
• End

1963 January 25   to   1984 November 22

Observing the Moon

The Moon is the easiest object in the sky to observe, since it's big and bright but not so bright that special precautions are needed to avoid blindness. On the other hand, to many people it is the most boring subject in the sky, since it doesn't do anything. There used to be a very important job for amateurs with the inclination to devote a lot of time and painstaking work on charting the Moon and producing maps, because most professional astronomers looked further afield. But the Apollo programme changed all that, since really good lunar maps were essential before landings could be contemplated. In addition, the pictures

Below: Past and future eclipse paths in the Northern Hemisphere

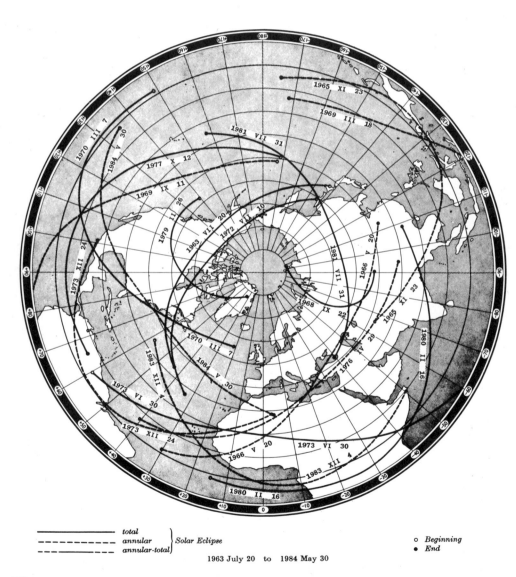

	total	
	annular	Solar Eclipse
	annular-total	

1963 July 20 to 1984 May 30

○ Beginning
● End

available from lunar orbital satellites are far better than any view you can obtain using a modest telescope, and they include pictures of the far side of the Moon, which is never visible from Earth.

It really is hard to see the point of anyone nowadays going to the trouble of making their own drawings of lunar features, except for their own amusement or as a challenge—'because it's there'.

That may sound depressing, but it shouldn't be really, for since there is no longer any need for amateurs to produce lunar charts you can contemplate the glories of our neighbour happily, without any guilt feeling that perhaps you ought to be doing something useful instead of just sitting back and enjoying the scenery.

Right: The moon (amateur photograph)

The scenery is certainly worth enjoying, especially at times when the Sun casts long shadows across the face of the Moon. At full Moon, when the Sun shines straight down into craters and onto mountains, the Moon looks flat and boring. But with shadows to bring out the relief, the views can be spectacular.

You can easily pick out interesting looking craters from any atlas of the Moon, and although you have no hope of seeing any traces of man's activity, it is sobering to look at the sites where the Apollo landings were made. But all this is strictly tourist stuff, for relaxation only.

Left: Close up of the Copernicus region of the moon photographed from Mt. Wilson using a 100" reflector

Right: A 6" Newtonian reflector telescope handmade by an amateur

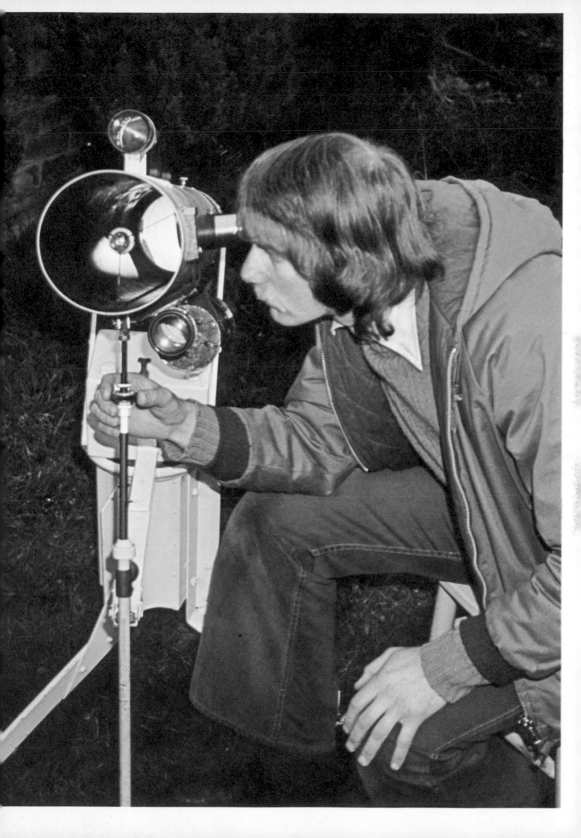

Above: The interior of
Copernicus photographed
from Lunar Orbiter II
approximately 28.4 miles
above the surface of the
moon. Left: The moon
photographed from Lick
Observatory with a 36"
refractor

Occultations

When the tourist vistas pall, you might like to try *using* the Moon as
a piece of astronomical equipment. I have already mentioned solar
eclipses, and although these are rare the Moon does often pass in
front of some other interesting object. You might guess that the
Moon passes over, or occults, many bright stars each night. But
you would be wrong. To the naked eye, there are only about 3,000
visible stars, and the Moon covers only half a degree on the sky. So
an occultation of a bright star is rare enough to be worthy of note,
but common enough that you don't need the patience of a saint to
observe one.

Lists of forthcoming occultations are available from amateur
astronomical societies, but although they can be predicted accurately, they cannot always be predicted precisely, since, you may
be surprised to learn, astronomers do not know the exact path the
Moon is going to follow across the sky.

Of course, the predictions are pretty good. But if you take care to
watch stars wink out as the Moon passes in front of them, and use
a stopwatch to time the occultation to better than a second, you
can make a very real contribution to improving our knowledge of
the orbit of the Moon.

The Moon also occults planets, and unlike stars these fade away
slowly as the edge of the Moon (the limb) passes across the disc of
the planet. A star just snaps out, because it seems a point of light to
us since it is so far away. This sudden snapping out, incidentally, is
proof that there is no atmosphere to speak of on the Moon, since a
lunar atmosphere would make a star being occulted twinkle and
fade out more slowly.

Overleaf: The Orion
Constellation from Hawaii,
with a guided Nikon F
camera at f1.4 with 30mm
exposure

57

Lunar occultations are now of very great interest to the newest branches of astronomy, since they can be used to pin down the locations of radio sources and X-ray stars very accurately. That is really beyond the scope of astronomy as a hobby, but it is interesting that the identification of the first known quasar was made with the aid of lunar occultations, and that a special X-ray satellite designed to take advantage of this phenomenon is planned by the European Space Agency (ESA).

Planets can also occult stars, and in these cases the flickering of the star as it disappears and reappears provides useful information about the atmosphere of the planet. Venus and Jupiter in particular have been studied in this way, and although such occurrences are rare they are correspondingly valuable.

On rarer occasions still, a planet may occult another planet. Venus occulted Mars in 1590 and Mercury in 1737, but there seems no prospect of another event of this kind in the near future.

Eclipses of the Moon itself occur when, as seen from the Moon, the Earth occults the Sun. Such a phenomenon would be of great interest to an observer on the Moon—but really, to astronomers on Earth the passage of the Moon through the Earth's shadow is a pretty dull affair. Perhaps in our lifetimes there will be amateur astronomers on the Moon, taking advantage of such occasions for special studies of the behaviour of the Earth's atmosphere. But until we are in a position to observe Earth regularly from space, we must turn our attention to the other planets of the Solar System, some of which are, after the Sun and Moon, as yet the brightest and most easily observed astronomical objects in the sky.

5 The Rest of the Solar System

Once again, as in the case of the Moon, the developments of the space age have made many of the mapping activities of amateurs redundant, where most of the planets of the Solar System are concerned. But that does not mean that the sight of, say, Mars is not worth the attention of the amateur; indeed, from the point of view of the astronomical hobbyist, looking at Mars can be even more intriguing in the light of the discoveries made by space vehicles.

The planets fall naturally into two groups, the **inner planets** (Mercury, Venus, Earth and Mars) which are small, rocky and closer to the Sun, and the **outer planets** (Jupiter, Saturn, Neptune and Uranus) which are large, gaseous and further away from the Sun. Tiny Pluto, the ninth planet, might seem to fall outside this pattern, being small and rocky but distant from the Sun; in fact, Pluto is probably a moon which has escaped from one of the gas giants, so it's not too surprising that it does not fit the pattern.

The inner planets

Of the inner planets, **Mercury** and **Venus** have orbits between that of the Earth and the Sun. Mercury's distance from the Sun averages only 36 million miles (about a third of the Sun-Earth distance) and the planet is very hard to observe. Space vehicles sent past Mercury show it to be superficially rather like our Moon, small, cratered and with very little atmosphere. Quite frankly, with a small telescope Mercury just is not worth the bother. The same is almost true of Venus. After the Sun and Moon, Venus is at times the brightest object in the sky, and very splendid to the naked eye observer. Unfortunately, even a giant telescope adds little to the naked eye view.

The reason for this is that Venus is veiled by clouds so that no surface features can ever be seen. These clouds seem to contain carbon dioxide, and the planet is also very hot, as space probes have revealed. The unveiling of Venus remains a task for future space probes, not for the amateur astronomer with his Earth-based telescope. But it is worth looking at Venus from time to time in order to see how its phases vary as it moves around the Sun.

We can only see these phases because Venus moves in an orbit between the Sun and the orbit of the Earth. When Venus is on the far side of the Sun, we can see the whole face—half the planet—reflecting sunlight as a small disc. When Venus lies almost exactly between the Earth and the Sun, only one edge is illuminated. This appears as a crescent, but much larger than the disc of 'full Venus' because the planet is much closer to Earth when the crescent is visible.

Midway between these extremes, of course, when Venus, the Sun and Earth form a right-angled triangle, we can see half of the illuminated face, which appears midway in size between the full and crescent Venus. As you can see, when Venus is at its closest to us, and the image in the telescope is biggest, we can see least of the planet! Fortunately there are no other planets between us and the Sun to be obscured in this exasperating way.

Left: Crescent Venus
photographed with a 200″
telescope. Even with this
instrument the results are,
to say the least, unexciting

Moving out from Venus, the next planet is the double system of Earth and our Moon. This would be a fascinating astronomical object to any observer elsewhere in the Solar System. Earth is the only planet which has just one moon and, as moons go, ours is remarkably large compared with the parent planet. Earth-Moon really would look like a double planet to an observer on Mars. But what does Mars look like to observers on Earth?

Although the orbit of **Mars** lies wholly outside that of the Earth, every two years the planets are on the same side of the Sun, in 'op-position', and for a few weeks Mars can be seen quite well through

Right: Saturn—the most
beautiful object in the Solar
System

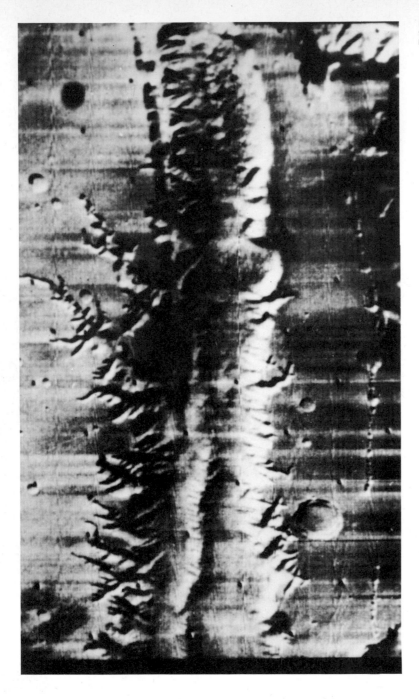

even a modest telescope. Because the orbits of the planets are not exactly circular, the distance between them at opposition may be as much as 60 million miles or as little as 35 million miles.

Curiously, Mars spins on its axis once every 24 hours 37 minutes, so that its day is very similar to ours. But there are few other similarities. The atmosphere is thin by our standards, and the planet is very cool. But it remains possible that some form of life may exist on Mars.

There is little chance of this being intelligent life; close flyby of space-probes shows Mars to be cratered and with great deserts, showing no sign of any organized activity. Indeed, the whole planet is pretty dead at present. But it may not always be quite like that.

The pictures from space vehicles such as Mariner 9 show very clear evidence of erosion on Mars, with what seem to be deltas and other features characteristic of running water—but the water is not there now. One explanation of this, put forward by the American astronomer Carl Sagan, is that although Martian water is today locked up as ice, below the ground or in the polar caps, it may be that from time to time some extra heating from the Sun allows the ice to melt. Carbon dioxide, which in its solid form 'dry ice' covers the Martian poles at present, would also be released by heating. According to Sagan, this would make the atmosphere thicker and allow water to flow. He can even provide a possible time scale for these changes, with Mars spending thousands of years in each kind of state, as its orbit around the Sun varies over the millenia. And just possibly when this strange Martian 'spring' occurs—if it ever occurs—then spores now dormant may spring into life and spread vegetation across the red planet.

It's an intriguing picture, but unfortunately we will never see it, even if Sagan's ideas are correct. What we can see through a small telescope is a distinctly reddish disc with white polar caps. These caps change in size with the Martian seasons but, in spite of the romantic ideas of an earlier generation of astronomers, there is no evidence at all that Martian people have built great canals to carry the water from the icecaps to equatorial regions. Indeed, only the small residual caps left in summer actually contain much water, the dramatic spread and retreat of the temporary parts of the caps being almost entirely caused by freezing and evaporation of carbon dioxide.

Once again, there is nothing really useful the amateur can contribute to the study of Mars today. In fact, thanks to Mariner 9, there is now a complete map of the planet available from NASA. With a great deal of patience and experience, you might be able to produce drawings indicating how features change, but there seems little point even in this activity (except for your own pleasure). Although features do change, it is now pretty clear that the cause of these changes is the occurrence of great dust storms, and not any real change in the surface features of the planet. By and large, then, the inner planets are a bit disappointing. The only worthwhile one to observe would be the Earth-Moon system—but we live on that one! All is not lost however; the gas giants well justify intensive study.

The outer planets

Between Mars and Jupiter there is a large gap in the Solar System's layout, in which many small objects, the minor planets, orbit. These are the most boring of all the members of the Solar

System to the casual observer; merely cosmic junk, a minor planet or **asteroid** may look like a faint star through your telescope, but you can tell that it is not because it will move, if not visibly over a few hours, then certainly to a noticeable degree by the next night. Ignore them.

But whatever you do, don't ignore **Jupiter,** the biggest planet of the Solar System. Jupiter never gets as close to us as 350 million miles, yet it is the next brightest object in the sky after Venus and (on the rare occasions of its closest approach) Mars. Late in 1974, Mars and Jupiter could both be seen high in the sky for a period of many weeks, and in spite of the great distance to Jupiter and the impressive appearance of Mars, the giant planet still looked the more important of the two, even to the naked eye.

Through a telescope Jupiter is even more impressive. A yellowish-brown disc, with streaks or bands, and rather flattened at the poles, Jupiter is accompanied by four satellites easily visible through a small telescope, and a host of others. I say 'host' since the number of Jovian satellites known is still being increased as more are discovered from time to time; but the total is more than a dozen. With anything except the smallest telescopes, more detailed patterns of wisps, bright areas and spots can be seen, including the famous **Great Red Spot.**

This spot, unlike most of the other features, is more or less permanent, and has been visible since at least 1631, although it became more conspicuous in 1878 and remains rather spectacular. At various times it has been suggested that the spot may be the site of a continuing volcanic eruption, or some kind of solid island floating in the Jovian clouds. The former idea can be ruled out, since it is now thought that Jupiter probably is not solid at all, but just gets denser toward the centre, remaining chiefly hydrogen gas right through.

The latest explanation of the coloration of Jupiter, including the Great Red Spot, is that long chains of organic molecules called polymers are built up in the soup of Jupiter's atmosphere. These polymers are rather like the ones used in the plastic industry on Earth; and one explanation of how they form is that chemical reactions take place during the wave of heat and compression of a thunder shock accompanying Jovian lightning. In that picture, the Great Red Spot is a plastic-wrapped thunderstorm!

If Jupiter is gas all the way through, then it's more like a star than a solid planet. Indeed, given a bit more mass Jupiter would have been big enough to become a star in its own right, since the pressure at the centre would have been enough for nuclear reactions to begin. Because of its gaseous nature, the planet does not rotate as a solid body, all at one speed, but at different speeds in different latitudes. In the Jovian tropics, the 'day' is 9 hours $50\frac{1}{2}$ minutes long, but at high latitudes it is 5 minutes longer.

Below: An amateur photograph of Jupiter

In addition, individual features may move at their own speeds. One, called the South Tropical Disturbance, was visible in the early part of this century moving around rather faster than the Great Red Spot, so that it actually passed the spot several times!

These individual features are the best to concentrate on for amateur study of Jupiter. Very few people are skilled enough to produce good drawings of the whole disc in the limited time

Above: Jupiter photographed with a 200″ telescope: showing the satellite, Ganymede and shadow, and Great Red Spot

available as features move across the planet, and it's much more valuable to concentrate on particular interesting regions, or to concentrate on one narrow band of latitudes at a time.

Because of the variations in the rotation rates of different features, it is even important to time their passage across the visible disc, and the accuracy needed is only to within a minute or so, not the split second accuracy needed for occultation work.

Like so much of astronomy, for this to be a worthwhile hobby you must have contact with other astronomers. You can work on your own, but there is also a time to meet and discuss ideas and techniques. There are many societies to join and ways to make contact, as described at the end of the book. So don't be daunted or put off by the apparent complexity of the task of recording observations in this way. Of course you won't be able to do much more than admire the Jovian scenery at first, but in time, with the aid of the contacts you will establish, you will be able to make a very valuable contribution to the accumulated work of Jupiter watchers around the world.

For the first time in our quick view of the planets we have found one that really can be a full-time hobby in itself. Jupiter has now been visited by two Pioneer spacecraft, and more visits are planned. But the planet is so big, so completely different from our own planet, and so poorly understood even now that it seems very unlikely that these visits will make amateur work redundant in the way that previous spaceprobes have made most amateur work on the inner planets redundant.

Most of those factors which make Jupiter so fascinating also apply to the other gas giants. But by the time we get past Jupiter the distances involved are beginning to be so great that observation with amateur equipment is severely restricted. Of course, Jupiter is especially interesting as the biggest of all the planets in the Solar System, and it's fortunate for those who make a hobby of astronomy that Jupiter is not in the orbit of Neptune, and Neptune in Jupiter's orbit! But even granted the difficulties of long range observation, the other gas giants are worth more than passing interest.

If Jupiter is the biggest planet, **Saturn** is surely the most beautiful. Smaller than Jupiter, with an equatorial diameter of 119,700 km compared with Jupiter's 142,100 km, Saturn possesses a glorious ring system, unique in our Solar System. With the rings as well, the system, easily visible through your telescope, is more than twice as wide as the planet alone and this broad ring system shows well defined structure.

Most of the remarks about observing Jupiter apply to Saturn, although the planet seems rather quieter and there are fewer interesting features to study. There is not a great deal to contribute to the present day understanding of the rings, which have already been well studied. The vital question of just what they are made of

Left: An amateur photo of Saturn showing the rings

Above: Saturn and its six inner satellites. The long exposure needed to photograph the satellites has burnt out the image of Saturn and its rings

is only likely to be answered when spaceprobes reach Saturn, and the first of these, Pioneer 11, is now on its lonely way to the ringed planet, having already flown past Jupiter and sent back a wealth of information and pictures at the end of 1974. Interestingly, Pioneer 11 has used Jupiter's gravitational field to swing itself around and on to Saturn, by the so-called 'gravitational slingshot'. Even with this aid, however, the spacecraft will not reach Saturn until 1979, and as yet NASA scientists have not decided whether to risk targetting Pioneer 11 to pass right through the rings.

Such a route is quite feasible, however, since the rings are extremely thin, possibly only around 10 miles in thickness, and are almost certainly made up of separate chunks of rock or frozen 'icebergs' of methane and similar compounds.

But although you may not contribute anything new to the study of Saturn's rings, they present a changing aspect of great interest to the casual observer. Because of the relative movement of the Earth and Saturn, sometimes we see the rings edge on (when they are just about invisible), sometimes from an angle 'above' the ring plane, sometimes from 'below' the plane, and of course at all intermediate positions. There are also ten satellites of Saturn known, and if you are very lucky you might see one of these superimposed against the line of the ring system, in its edge on or closed situation, looking like a bead on a wire.

Far out beyond Saturn lies **Uranus,** about half as big as the ringed planet and too distant to be seen in detail with a small telescope. You should be able to see the disc of this planet, three times as distant as Jupiter, but little else. There are five known satellites of Uranus, and you could see two of these with a moderate reflector—10-inches or more—but there is very little you can do except note that they exist.

The same is true of **Neptune,** much the same size as Uranus but so distant that it never comes within 2,675 million miles of Earth. The last known planet in the Solar System is Pluto, only discovered in 1930 and so small and distant that very little is known about it at all. The only point in looking for **Pluto** at all is to say that you have seen the most distant planet in the Solar System, but in fact because of its elliptical orbit Pluto sometimes passes within the orbit of Neptune, and just now (until the end of this century) Neptune is the furthest planet from the Sun, so even that satisfaction is likely to be muted.

Comets

Not really to be included in the same category as planets, but still members of our Solar System, comets can be well worth investigating. We are now well overdue for a good bright comet, visible to the naked eye and producing a spectacular display across a sizeable fraction of the sky. The unfortunate fanfare of publicity for the inoffensive Comet Kohoutek in 1973 made many people aware of what a comet can be like, only to dash their hopes. But, armed with a telescope, the astronomical hobbyist need not wait for the greatest comets; indeed, Comet Kohoutek itself would have been interesting to observe with a moderate reflector.

A comet is basically a central condensation with a long filmy tail streaming out from it. This tail is so insubstantial, in spite of its appearance, that it is pushed away from the nucleus by the magnetic field and particles which stream away from the Sun. I have already mentioned something of the orbits of comets, and their relationship with meteors, in Chapter 2. Many periodic comets are known, and can be found from tables published by astronomical societies. Studies of the changing patterns of the tail of any comet are of great importance as an aid in developing astronomers' understanding of just how the tail interacts with the solar wind of particles moving outward across the Solar System. Non-periodic comets, like Kohoutek, are usually picked up in good time for the word to be spread so that amateurs can contribute to their investigation. But the big excitement about comets for the hobbyist must still be the opportunity of astronomical immortality that is provided to the discoverer of a new comet.

Because comets do appear unexpectedly, patience in sweeping the skies rather than possession of a great telescope is the key to

Left: Halley's Comet, photographed on 31 May, 1910

70

Above: Comet Arend
Roland, on 29 April, 1957

discovering them. You really do have to sweep patiently across a chosen region of the sky, waiting for something unusual to come into view. You may never find anything, but perhaps the effort will be worthwhile if you use the opportunity to keep an eye on other interesting objects in that region of the sky. On the other hand, some amateurs have developed a knack of finding comets, and are well known as a result.

The study of comets, like the study of Jupiter, can take up all your time once you begin to take it seriously. So, after the disappointments of some of the planets, we already have three areas of specialization for the prospective hobbyist who is armed with a telescope: the Sun (especially sunspots); Jupiter and its varying details (including the Great Red Spot); and comets. And we still have not left the Solar System!

6 Beyond the Solar System

For the amateur, the problem of observing stars and other objects beyond the Solar System is chiefly one of getting enough light into his telescope to make the effort worthwhile. One of the most important areas of astronomy is the study of the **spectra** of different objects—stars, nebulae, or whatever. But to obtain a spectrum, the light entering the observer's telescope has to be split up by a prism into its constituent colours. If the light is faint to start with, each bit of the spectrum will be too faint for any measurements to be worthwhile.

This kind of work is not beyond the amateur, especially if he builds up gradually from studying spectra of bright objects—even the planets of the Solar System. But if you are going to do this on a worthwhile basis you must be a really dedicated astronomer—as an amateur, in some ways you need to be more dedicated than the professionals—and this kind of 'serious' amateur astronomy really goes rather beyond the kind of entertaining hobby which astronomy can be to many more people with a lot less effort. So what is there for the hobbyist, rather than the dedicated amateur or professional astronomer, to get out of the vast bulk of the Universe beyond the Solar System?

Nebulae

First of all, there are once again lots of pretty sights to see. We live in a fairly ordinary region of the lens-shaped congregation of stars which is our Galaxy, and our Galaxy is nothing special among the thousands and millions of other galaxies scattered about the Universe. The great nebula in **Andromeda** is, in fact, another ordinary galaxy which happens to be rather close to us, and by turning our telescopes that way we can get a rough idea of how our own family of stars would look from the outside. The **Magellanic Clouds,** the sky marks of the southern hemisphere, are also separate galaxies, small irregularly shaped satellites of our own Milky Way system.

Closer to home, there are many tourist attractions even in our ordinary corner of an ordinary galaxy. The nebula in **Orion**, for example, is a cloud of gas and dust within our Galaxy, and this may be the kind of place where new stars are born out of the matter between the stars. This particular nebula is particularly easy to photograph, as we will see in Chapter 7, and indeed the whole constellation of Orion provides plenty of scope for investigating what goes on beyond the Solar System.

The other nebula to which any newcomer to astronomy must soon turn his telescope is the famous **Crab Nebula** in Taurus. It's a bit confusing that astronomers use the name 'nebula' for so many different kinds of object—almost anything that is not obviously a star, in fact, but that's just because of the trouble early observers had in distinguishing the difference between the different kinds of object in the sky. As we have already seen, a 'nebula' can be a whole galaxy of stars beyond our own Galaxy, or it can be a cloud of dust and gas inside our Galaxy where new stars are being born.

Right: The Great Nebula in Orion

But another kind of nebula marks the site of a dead star, and the Crab comes in this category.

In 1054 AD, Chinese astronomers noticed that a star in Taurus had brightened to rival anything in the sky except the Sun and Moon, for a short time. You can imagine the superstitious awe in which such events were regarded then; but we now know that this was a **supernova**, an explosion in which a star gives up the ghost, not with a whimper but with a bang, as it becomes unstable at the end of the phase of its life as an ordinary star.

Such supernova explosions are not too common—most stars quietly fade away in rather less spectacular deaths. But when a supernova explosion does occur it produces a blast of gas expanding outwards, and leaves some interesting 'cinders' behind.

The Crab Nebula is the still expanding gas cloud of that supernova explosion watched by the Chinese astronomers more than 900 years ago. Of course, the actual explosion occurred long before that; the Crab is so far away that light from it takes 6,000 years to reach our Solar System—and any intelligent observers 950 light years away from us in the opposite direction from the Crab will still be seeing it as an ordinary star. They will see the supernova explosion in another 30 years or so, by our reckoning!

Inside the Crab Nebula, at the site of the original explosion, there remains a tiny, spinning star which emits radio waves, X-rays and enough light to be still visible, through a large telescope, as an optical star. At all these wavelengths, this 'cinder' pulses every 33 milliseconds—it is known as the Crab pulsar, code named NP0531. All this activity, and the relative proximity of the Crab (6,000 light years is just next door by astronomical standards), mean that the Crab is just about the most intensively studied object in the sky, and astronomers sometimes joke that their science can be divided into two parts, the study of the Crab and the study of everything else!

Left: A supernova in the galaxy NGC 7331 observed in 1959 —top: the galaxy before the supernova explosion; bottom: at its brightest the supernova rivalled the brightness of all the rest of the stars in the galaxy put together

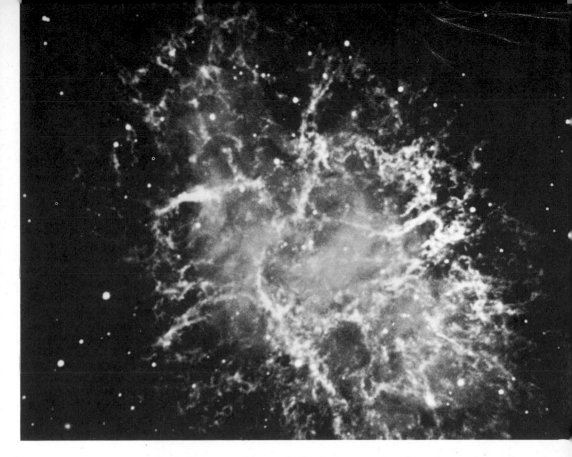

Above: The Crab Nebula, relic of a supernova which was visible on Earth in 1054 AD

The amateur with a small telescope can, of course, only study the nebula itself. But even that is something more than a pretty sight. Because of the continuing activity of the central pulsar, energy is still being poured out into the nebula from the centre. That is why, even after the best part of 1,000 years, the Crab is still such a prominent feature of the heavens. And it also means that the filaments in the nebula, especially those near the central star, are being agitated. This agitation can sometimes be detected as wisps which move forward and back as they receive jolts of energy from the pulsar. It's still not clear exactly how this happens (a few people have doubts about whether it really happens at all) and the changes certainly are not predictable. To my mind nebulae are, for the hobbyist, just pretty sites to be admired. For those who want to do more than admire the view, we must turn our attention elsewhere.

Double stars

If you can't make worthwhile observations of stars which don't do anything except sit there glowing faintly (at least, faintly as viewed from Earth), the obvious thing to do is to study stars which vary visibly over a timescale that fits in with the frequency with which you can make observations. Some stars are really variable, as we will see in the next section. But some of them only seem to vary, because they are really double stars—and these are among the most fascinating objects for the amateur astronomer.

A few stars look 'double' simply because they lie in almost the same direction, from our Solar System, although they may be at vastly different distances. But some stars really are physically associated in double, or more complex, systems.

In such a genuine binary, or double star, system, the two stars revolve about their mutual centre of mass under the physical binding of their gravitational fields. Even a small telescope will show you hundreds of such pairs of stars, and it may well be that this is the common state of stars—our own Solar System, with just one star and a few planets, may be something of a freak by astronomical standards. Binary stars have been of crucial importance to the development of astronomy, because careful study of their changes can tell us what the masses of the stars are—there is absolutely no direct way of working out the mass of a star which sits on its own in space. And because there are so many binaries known, and some of them have not received a lot of attention because they seem relatively insignificant, there is even scope for the amateur to make the appropriate measurements in some cases.

The separation of the stars in a binary, as viewed from Earth, is measured in 'seconds of arc'. For comparison, the Moon covers half a degree on the sky, about 1,800 seconds of arc. So a separation of a couple of seconds of arc is rather on the small side by terrestrial standards. The separation we see varies, of course, as the stars swing around each other. And this variation tells us about the orbit and masses of the binary pair. The astronomer M. P. Candy, writing in the book *Practical Amateur Astronomy* (which I strongly recommend) says 'that there is plenty of scope for the amateur to work in this field. But he must exercise quite as much stubborn perseverance and attention to detail as the professional, if he wants his results to be accepted.' So you have been warned—but still, there are very few areas of science where the complete amateur, working at weekends perhaps, really can produce results which will be welcomed and used by professionals at the forefront of research today. You will find out just how to set about this exacting task in standard reference books, such as those mentioned in the Further Reading section. But if that does not appeal (or even if it does), take a look at some of the more spectacular visual binaries.

The best sights are the pairs in which the two 'components' are different colours. **Beta Cygni**, in the constellation Cygnus, contains a yellow star with a blue-green companion, easily visible separately even with a 6-inch reflector. For a whole family of stars, turn your telescope towards **Epsilon Lyrae**, which lies close to the bright marker star Vega (which is almost overhead at the latitude of England in early Summer). This star is visible even to the naked eye as a binary—but a small telescope reveals that each member of that pair is itself a binary, and spectroscopic analysis shows that one of these four stars is itself a binary.

Many more binaries are listed in *Norton's Star Atlas* as 'interesting objects'. Armed with this atlas, the casual observer can spend many hours on a guided tour of the heavens, and this indispensable aid to the observer is also inexpensive, so there is no need for me to list more interesting binaries here.

Variable stars

The 'interesting' double stars mentioned so far do not actually seem to vary in brightness—only the position of the two (or more) stars relative to each other on the sky varies, as they orbit one another. Some binaries are arranged so that they sometimes eclipse each other, as seen from Earth; but this only occurs for the relatively few objects which have an orbital plane that cuts our line of sight. Stars like **Algol** and **Beta Lyrae** come in this category, and change visibly to the naked eye—look them up in *Norton's Star Atlas* and check for yourself. But what of really variable stars, which genuinely fluctuate in brightness?

The most important variables are known as **Cepheids**, named after the archetype Delta Cephei. These stars vary regularly, and the period of variation depends on the real brightness of the star—its 'intrinsic magnitude'. This is very useful, since just by measuring the period of a Cepheid, calculating its intrinsic magnitude and comparing this with its apparent brightness in the sky, we can find out how far away the star is. Indeed, this method is the key first step used by astronomers in determining stellar distances. Cepheid periods generally lie in the range from a few days to seven weeks.

A similar but more rapid variation occurs in **RR Lyrae** stars, over periods of 2 to 30 hours, while for longer periods we can study the **long-period variables** which change over periods of 70 days to 2 years. There are also **irregular variables**, which change repeatedly but erratically, and **cataclysmic variables**—nova and supernova explosions—which vary only once, but rather impressively.

Betelgeuse, in Orion, is worth a look from time to time. This star varies with an approximate period of four or five years, but it's really an irregular variable; its changes can be followed with the naked eye. But why should stars change in these ways?

For Cepheids at least, the answer seems to be that the star 'breathes' in and out, and the same is probably true of RR Lyrae stars. But all the good bright short-period variables have been thoroughly studied already, and except for satisfaction of your personal curiosity they can be ignored. Long period variables are another matter, however, and here again the amateur can contribute observations which will be welcomed by professional astronomers.

The same need for scrupulous accuracy applies and again, as a first step towards this, study the relevant chapter of *Practical Amateur Astronomy.* And, of course, observations of irregular variables are equally important. But one word of warning—do make sure you are observing the star you think you are! That is not as silly as it sounds, since although with practice you can be sure of the location of the pattern of stars (the starfield) viewed through your telescope, the less experience you have the harder it is to be sure.

The best method is to use stellar 'stepping stones' as a guide. Start without the telescope, and identify the bright stars near the variable you are looking for from your star atlas. Then sweep from one clear pattern to the next with your telescope, making comparisons with the chart, and sneaking up on the object of interest.

Here is one case where life is definitely easier for the modern professional astronomer. The new Anglo-Australian Telescope at Siding Spring is computer-controlled to such an extent that the operator just punches in the co-ordinates of the star to be studied, sits back, and lets the computer steer the telescope to the precise point of interest! For the amateur, however, the careful approach, together with star charts (usually obtainable through amateur societies) is essential.

Mention of Australia perhaps makes this an appropriate place to point out how little is known about the entire sweep of the southern skies, compared with what we know about the northern hemispheres. Any amateurs 'down under' have even more scope than their northern colleagues to make valuable contributions to astronomy, simply because there are so many more telescopes, amateur and professional, in the north.

When it comes to exploding stars, however, you need luck whether it's north or south of the equator that you do your observing. A **nova** occurs when a star, at the end of its life as a nuclear fusion power plant, becomes unstable and blasts its outer layers away into space. Such events are not exactly common on the human scale of things—a score or so that were visible to the naked eye have been recorded this century, and rather more of the fainter novae. But they are common enough to make it worthwhile to look out for them, and, as is the case with comet searchers, the amateur with a keen interest in the heavens has as good a chance as the professional astronomer of being the first to spot such an event.

Whether or not you discover a nova yourself, however, be sure to take advantage of any opportunity to observe one that does occur. The spectacular brightening is generally followed by a slower decline in brightness, with perhaps lesser flaring occurring after the main event. Novae can develop odd coloration, conspicuous even through a small telescope, and the sites of old novae are sometimes of interest because they can develop visible clouds of gas and dust—the remains of the outer layers of the star, expanding into space.

Supernovae, as the name suggests, are even brighter stellar explosions, and we don't really know exactly why some stars should have such spectacular endings. The Crab supernova has already been mentioned. It is rare for a supernova to be that close and appear so brightly in our skies, but according to the best astronomical guesses we are likely to have a supernova explosion in our Galaxy once or twice every hundred years. On that 'average', we are overdue for a telescopically spectacular supernova—and for a fairly nearby one, if it comes to that. So it just may be that there will be one such event within your lifetime.

If you are already attracted to the idea of immortality through discovering a comet, you might like to keep your eyes open for novae (and perhaps a supernova?) as well. There's little chance that you'll be the lucky one—but then, someone must be! Good luck; and be sure to let me know if you do discover one.

7 Astronomical Photography

For the more casual astronomical hobbyist, photography can be the most pleasant and rewarding aspect of astronomy. There is plenty of scope for detailed, painstaking work involving much time and effort—there always is in astronomy! But the ability of the camera to see more than the human eye, and to see the same things in a different way, means that very pleasing results can be obtained with a minimum of astronomical effort or knowledge. You have more work to do in the darkroom, but to my mind that is amply compensated for by not needing to spend so many long, frozen hours outside. And photographic processing is hardly a daunting task, even to someone as notoriously impractical as myself.

In some ways, this chapter should perhaps have followed directly from Chapter Two, on 'Naked Eye Observations'. For although specialist astronomical equipment, such as a telescope, is essential to develop astronomical photography as a worthwhile hobby, the first steps can be taken with no specialist equipment at all—just any ordinary camera that has a time-exposure feature. Indeed, many of the pictures in this book were taken by amateurs using very simple photographic equipment.

The fact that the stars appear to describe circles around the poles as the Earth rotates is hardly a new discovery, and the evidence is easy to photograph: just lay your camera so that it points towards the pole (a tripod is, of course, desirable, but you can do just as well by leaning the camera against a convenient wall or a brick) and take a time exposure over a couple of hours. Provided you've chosen a dark, cloudless night, the result will be a picture showing a series of circular trails around the pole. And although that may be nothing new, I bet you will get a big kick out of doing the 'experiment' yourself and seeing the result. I certainly did!

Below: A trail of stars around the Pole star; direct photography by amateur Brian Jobson: 10 minute exposure, fixed camera at f2, HP4 film

Still without any special astronomical equipment, you can move on from pretty pictures of bright constellations (a ten minute exposure of Orion, the Plough or the Southern Cross will produce a recognizable picture, only slightly blurred by the apparent movement of the stars) to studying meteors and artifical satellites. The observations are much the same as those you would make with the naked eye or binoculars (see Chapter Two), but less of a strain on the eyes and the muscles in the back of your neck. Photographing satellite trails is pretty dull in itself, but may be very useful if you are involved in some special study of these objects. But meteors provide scope both for the casual hobbyist and the more dedicated amateur observer.

Below: The Orion constellation, direct photography by amateur Chris Mitchell: 15 secs at f1.4 TRI-X film

Right: The Plough, star trails taken with a fixed camera by amateur Clive Nanson: 5 minute exposure at f3.5 TRI-X rated at 800 ASA

Photographing meteors

When a meteor shower is expected, direct the camera towards the point in the sky from which they should appear to be coming (the **radiant**), open the shutter, and go away to have a cup of coffee, watch TV or make observations of something else with your telescope. After a couple of hours, close the shutter, wind the film on, and repeat. After processing, the end product should be a pattern of faint trails with, if you are lucky, one good bright meteor, or even a meteor that has exploded, having left its mark on your film.

For useful work, you have to give up the coffee and TV, because you should really watch the sky yourself to note the time at which any particularly bright meteor occurs. Then, if you are working with a colleague or two a dozen miles away, you can compare notes and photographs to find the height of the meteor, and its exact path, by **triangulation.** The calculations are very straightforward, and for this kind of work you are sure to have made contact with some local group of amateurs with relevant experience, so I will not give further details here.

The next step upwards in sophistication is also very simple. This is the provision of some kind of rotating shutter in front of the camera, turning at a known speed. When a meteor flashes across the sky, its trail will be broken up on the photograph by the repeated passage of the shutter, and will appear as a series of dots or dashes. Since the speed of the shutter's movement is known, you can easily work out the speed of the meteor from the length of each section of trail between the passages of the shutter. Again, devising a rotating shutter is simple, especially if you can talk to someone who has done it before.

Once you get really involved in this game, you might even participate in worldwide **fireball monitoring,** with only one extra item of equipment. For the fireball network, a camera with a 'fisheye' lens is essential, so that the entire visible hemisphere of the sky can be recorded on one photograph. That way, you can be sure of recording every meteor, and the hope is that, by triangulation from several stations, the network may enable astronomers to record not just meteors but meteorites—larger solid objects which don't burn up completely in the atmosphere but survive to leave a fragment which hits the Earth's surface. With a fireball network of this kind, maybe it will be possible to 'catch' meteorites, locate their landing place and collect them before they can be contaminated by organisms from Earth. This is obviously of great importance for finding out just what kind of molecules might exist in meteors in space, and especially whether the complicated 'organic' molecules that have been called the 'precursors of life' might have originated in space.

Unfortunately, there are snags even with this project. According to reliable reports, only one meteorite has yet been caught in this way. When the observers arrived at the triangulated landing position, a farm in North America, they were lucky enough to find, it being winter, a newly burnt hole in the snow and, at the bottom of the hole, meteorite fragments just as predicted. When the fragments were analysed, they were found to contain organic compounds just like those found in living things on Earth, and this caused great excitement—until someone took a careful look at the colour pictures that had been taken of the meteorite's snowy landing place. These showed a suspicious patch of yellow snow right by the hole made by the meteorite, and further tests showed that indeed the organic compounds had not come from space, but from the dog which lived on the farm!

But the fireball network is bound to strike lucky one day soon, and perhaps you will be a contributor to the big find. If you want to take good pictures of more remote objects, however, you will certainly need to start using more sophisticated equipment—but nothing too sophisticated unless you really want to.

Photography through a telescope

So far, the choice of camera for the observations I have described has been pretty wide. Now the choice is more restricted, but not to a prohibitive extent. For this kind of astronomical photography you really need to be able to see with your own eye just what the camera can 'see'. In other words, you must have a **single lens reflex camera.** For work with a telescope, you don't really need the camera's own lens so, to be more specific, you need *the body only* of a single lens reflex (SLR) camera. This might sound a problem in financial terms, if you are aware of the cost of the kind of SLR equipment used by professional news photographers and the like; but don't worry, you don't need anything so sophisticated.

The point is that this expensive equipment is designed to take pictures quickly, and with the right exposure, under a variety of different light conditions. That's where the expense comes in. But for astronomical work you want to time the exposures yourself, or use automatic exposures of at least several tenths of a second, so a shutter operating with wonderful automatic precision at a few hundredths of a second is unnecessary. And again, the lens system you will use will be your own telescope, so no expense is involved there. Indeed, the equipment you really need hardly fits the standard image of a camera: a box-like arrangement for holding film would do, and many people do build their own astronomical cameras. If you like that kind of do-it-yourself, by all means try it, with the aid of a couple of the books mentioned in the Further Reading. But a basic SLR body (which you can buy without a lens) could be got for less than £25 or $60 (Russian SLRs are cheap and rugged), and they are also widely available secondhand; so I have never felt the need to dabble in do-it-yourself camera building.

At the other extreme, it's possible to buy ready made special telescopes which are essentially camera systems. These **Schmidt cameras** are the best for astronomical photography, but they are not cheap, and you need to be really sure that you are going in for the game in a big way before you buy one. If you want to find out something about them (and their cost), glance through a few issues of the magazine *Sky and Telescope.* You will find many advertisements for Schmidt cameras, and probably several photographs taken with them.

Once you have your SLR body (or home-made camera), it must be attached to the telescope, joining on to the eyepiece tube. Suitable adaptors are generally readily available, and again it's a good thing (but not essential) to call on the advice of someone who has done it all before. The telescope is focused by viewing through the camera system (which is why an SLR is by far the best body for the job); the shutter must, of course, be operated using a long cable release, to avoid shaking the telescope/camera system. Indeed, if you want to be really fussy about shake, focus the telescope first, then cover the main objective lens by holding a piece of card in front of it before opening the shutter. Now, remove the cardboard screen for the beginning of the exposure, and replace it at the end, only operating the shutter again when the sky is 'blanked off'.

One other piece of equipment is essential for good photography through a telescope, and that is a **clock drive.** There is no way that you will be able to steer the telescope adequately by hand, while keeping the position of the image on the film precisely fixed. And, of course, you will need some **film,** but that is hardly specialized equipment. Kodak Plus X is a good choice, or something similar with an ASA rating between 100 and 150, and although faster films are supposed to be less desirable because they are more grainy and likely to suffer blemishes, I have used Tri X (ASA 400) with entirely satisfactory results. But don't take my word for it, or anybody else's. Film is so cheap, and approval of its qualities is so subjective, that it's best to try several different varieties for yourself and choose the one you like best. It's rather like choosing a Hi-Fi system; only you know what you like (but unfortunately Hi-Fi is a little too expensive to buy several and choose the best after a comparison!).

What to photograph

Every beginner seems to make the **Orion Nebula** his first target for photography through a telescope, and there are good reasons why you should do the same. The nebula is easy to find, fairly bright and particularly prominent at the red end of the spectrum where 'normal' film is more sensitive. Try a range of exposures, depending on the speed of your film, the extent to which you trust your clock drive, and your patience, starting at about 5 seconds and working upwards. If you like the results (and I'll be surprised if you don't) point your camera towards a few other nebulae and interesting objects and see how even a fairly short exposure brings out details you can never see by eye.

Colour snaps can be even more of a revelation, again because the film builds up its image steadily over the period of the exposure, whereas the human eye is saturated by a quick glimpse, and you will never see any more detail however long you stare at the sky. Again, try the Orion Nebula, using an ordinary film such as Kodacolor II; take a 10 minute exposure, using the clock drive of your telescope to steer the camera, but without using the telescope itself to enlarge the image. Try the same thing with the camera on an ordinary tripod, using faster colour film for a 10, 20 or 30 second exposure, and try photographing anything in sight, using ordinary colour film, through the same telescope/camera system as for the black and white photography described above. Some of the results will be rotten, but the good ones will make up for that, and you will soon learn for yourself which combinations of film and exposure are best for the results you want to achieve.

One important point is that although the kind of colour film used for your holiday snaps will record images of astronomical objects, this kind of 'colour negative' film (such as Kodacolor) goes through an extra stage of processing where the image is transferred on to a positive print. The exact colours that result depend to some extent on the whim of the printer; so for consistent results it is better to use 'Transparency' film, such as High Speed Ektachrome or GAF. If you do use a negative film, make sure you warn the printer what to expect—many will assume that what you think is a beautiful sky picture is some horrible mistake, and won't print it at all.

Because colour transparencies show changes in colour of astronomical objects so well, it's certainly worth taking regular pictures of the sky—without a telescope but with the aid of a simple cheap motor drive—just to see what turns up. Several valuable pre-discovery images of novae have been obtained in this way. ('Pre-discovery' means that the picture was taken some time before the nova brightened sufficiently to be recognized for what it was: it is essential to file such transparencies carefully with records of date and time if they are ever to be of any use other than as pretty pictures.)

Another stage in sophistication comes when three black and white pictures of the same object, taken through different filters, are combined to produce a colour photograph. This may sound like magic, but it's not; however, it is not something to be tried by the beginner. So having whetted your appetite by hinting about it, I will leave you to find out more from other sources (local society, books and so on) when you have become so adept at the kind of photography I have described above that you feel ready to move on to something a bit special.

Photographing the Solar System

Photographing **sunspots** is almost too easy, like shooting fish in a barrel, but the results can be very satisfying, especially if you neglect to tell your admirers how easy it was. The simplest method is to project the solar image onto a white screen in a dark enclosure and photograph the image. With a green or yellow-green filter to enhance the picture, the end product should easily be good enough to justify enlarging and hanging on the wall.

The **Moon** is undoubtedly the most popular target for amateur astronomer-photographers; but except for the pleasure of doing it yourself, and the obvious fascination of our nearest neighbour in

84

space, it is hard to see why—especially now that the excellent spaceprobe pictures are available. It may sound heretical to many dedicated amateur astronomers, but to my eye one lunar picture looks much the same as another (or, indeed, much the same as a Mariner 10 picture of Mercury!). And in the case of the Moon you get no benefit from the camera's ability to pull in more light than the human eye can use. I am not denying that the lunar landscape is fascinating, nor that it is worth looking at often through a telescope. But pictures of it I can live without.

Most of the planets are also fairly useless as targets for photography, for the same reasons that they are useless for telescopic observation (see Chapter 5). But **Mars** is worthwhile since, especially with an orange filter, surface markings can be brought out even with an exposure of less than a second. (Exact exposure depends, of course, on the telescopic set-up you are using; any figures I mention are only to be taken as a very rough guide, and you should try different combinations of film, magnification and so on until you find the best for your equipment.) The changing size of the polar caps on Mars can be recorded over a period of time.

As in the case of direct observation, **Jupiter** makes the best photographic subject in our Solar System. Fast colour film (for transparencies) can produce good pictures of Jupiter, showing the Great Red Spot to advantage. (It is also worth trying a colour transparency or two of Mars.) Again, the kind of exposure time relevant for all these pictures is in the range one to a few seconds, as opposed to several minutes.

A rather longer exposure is needed for **Saturn,** because it is so far away, and anything less than 5 seconds is unlikely to produce good results. But it is worth the slight extra effort involved if you can get a good picture of the famous rings.

All this kind of work soon palls, however, and unless you are working on a special project you won't spend much time photographing the planets. Photographing **comets** can be more rewarding, but needs the development of great skill in guiding the telescope while fairly long exposures are made, to bring out detail of these faint objects. Certainly not for the beginner, or casual astronomical hobbyist.

In my view, astronomical photography is the best aspect of amateur astronomy in terms of producing worthwhile results with minimum effort and expertise, and without great expense. I strongly recommend you to try it, and of course you are bound to dabble with photographing planets (even the Moon) for a while. But objects beyond the Solar System are so varied and fascinating that they can keep you occupied for as long as your interest in astronomy lasts. Nebulae, interestingly paired double stars, novae (if you are lucky) and even the satisfaction of producing pictures of other galaxies almost unimaginably distant from our own family of stars, are all there for the taking, and there is plenty of scope to develop new skills and expertise in colour work and to spend all your money on beautiful Schmidt cameras. Be warned—once the bug gets you, astronomical photography is not so much a hobby, more a way of life.

8 Radio Astronomy

The popular image of radio astronomy is a giant dish like those at Jodrell Bank in England or Arecibo in Puerto Rico. Nothing could be more remote from the realm of the amateur—but don't be fooled by this. If you have any aptitude for electronic and radio work at all, radio astronomy is a straightforward and rewarding hobby, which need not involve you in any great expense. Indeed, as the number of radio amateurs around indicates, it is much easier to build sophisticated radio equipment than sophisticated optical equipment. In addition, because radio astronomy is still in many ways a young science, there is more scope for worthwhile observations by amateurs—in some areas, at least. But on the other hand you do need some familiarity with things electronic; at the very simplest level, to 'see' anything by radio does require more than to 'see' something with an off-the-peg telescope.

Below: The 100m diameter, fully steerable radio telescope of the Max-Planck Institut for Radio Astronomy. This is the largest instrument of its kind at present operating anywhere in the world

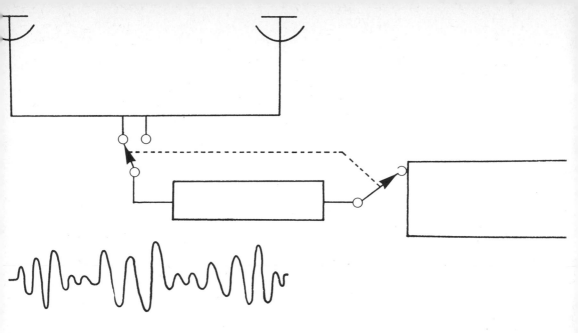

Above: A simplified diagram
of an interferometric
system: a two-antennae
interferometer, linked to a
receiver, which in turn feeds
the signals into a decoder
and chart recorder. Below is
a sample chart trace of the
radio noise received

Apparatus

For radio astronomy you need at least two, and preferably three, linked pieces of equipment. First, an **aerial** to pick up the signal from beyond the Earth's atmosphere. The simplest kind is a Yagi array, like a standard TV antenna, which is pointed towards the region of interest, rather like an optical telescope would be. The second most simple kind of antenna involves a basic rod (dipole) aerial with a reflector behind it—or a row of dipoles with a reflector behind them. Professionals use parabolic reflectors to focus the radio waves, just as optical telescopes use parabolic mirrors; but a simple sheet of metal with a right-angle bend in it (a 'corner reflector') is easier to make and pretty effective. Beyond these simple versions, it is possible to use combinations of aerials to build up an antenna system called an **interferometer.** This needs more space, and more expertise in building and running the equipment which combines the radio signal from each component aerial in the interferometer into a meaningful 'picture'. It is really beyond the scope of the beginner, and I will say no more about interferometry here. But remember that if you do take up radio astronomy and master the basics, there is plenty of scope for later sophistication.

The antenna system is no use, of course, without an **amplifier** to put the radio noise into a form where human senses can notice it; and it is almost essential to have some kind of recording system so that radio observations can be examined and analysed at leisure, not 'on the spot'. These two parts of the system are probably best purchased, perhaps from government surplus supplies, unless you already have some experience of radio work. The **recorder** most suited to the work would be a chart recorder in which an unrolling reel of paper is marked, like a graph, by a pen which responds to the intensity of the radio noise being received.

But the antenna system could well be built even by a complete beginner. For the very first steps, you can easily use a large TV antenna of the kind designed to fit on a roof or outside wall—or two or more such antennae coupled together.

Basic observations—the Sun
Now, there is no way that I can give you enough information, in the space available, to enable you to begin dabbling in radio work unless you already know some basic electronics. Besides, this book is supposed to be a guide to astronomy, not to electronic devices. So if you want to dabble in radio astronomy, but know nothing of these basics, don't read on yet. First of all, find out something about the fundamentals of radio (either from general books or from the particularly relevant books mentioned later). If you find the effort too great, or the mechanics of building and maintaining radio equipment too daunting, go back to optical astronomy and stick with it. But if you find the electronic side fascinating, or if you are already a convert to the joys of radio in a non-astronomical context, here are some pointers to start you on your way in radio astronomy.

The Sun is a delight to amateur radio astronomers, because its radio characteristics vary intriguingly over the solar cycle of activity. When there are few sunspots (Quiet Sun) the solar emissions are markedly different from those during more active parts of the sunspot cycle. The Sun emits over a broad range of frequencies, and observations can be made fairly easily over the whole range. But the lower the frequency, the bigger the space you need for your aerial systems. Starting out with a basic Yagi system, you are restricted to the higher frequency range of the solar radio spectrum; but everyone has to begin somewhere.

The kind of basic solar observation programme that can be rewarding should already be clear from the chapters devoted to optical astronomy. Just regular monitoring of solar emission over a chosen band of frequencies for a complete solar cycle will keep you well occupied for 11 years, especially since you should also make records of the sunspot activity and any sunspot groups visible at the time of your radio observations.

This is not as boring as it sounds, especially when unusual flares or spot groups can be seen to be associated with unusual radio activity, but of course no-one would really devote 11 years to such a project and nothing else! The obvious next step, from simply observing the activity of the Sun, is to record the **occultation** of another radio source, such as the Crab Nebula, by the Sun. Just as occultation of a star by Jupiter can tell us about Jupiter's atmosphere, so the occultation of a radio source by the Sun tells us about the extent and composition of the Sun's 'atmosphere'—the corona. The intensity of the signal from, say, the Crab slowly drops away as the occultation begins, and slowly rises afterwards. The more sophisticated your equipment is (in particular, the narrower the field of view, or 'beamwidth', of your antenna system), then the more information these occultations will reveal. This again is an area of astronomy where really first-class amateur observations can be of great use to the professionals.

Jupiter
The biggest planet in our Solar System is the only one you will be

able to detect by radio techniques, and you will need to step up a bit from the simplest antenna to get it at all. Generally, Jupiter transmits somewhere in the range 17 to 24 MegaHertz, but not always at exactly the same frequencies in this range. Together with the motion of the planet, this can make attempts at observing its radio emission frustrating—but correspondingly pleasing when they succeed. It can be done, but I would not advise anyone to try it early in their venture into radio astronomy, since you might get so fed up that you discard the whole idea of radio astronomy as a hobby. When you want to try it, I recommend the advice on aerials in the book *Practical Amateur Astronomy* (see Further Reading); meanwhile, keep it simple.

Beyond the Solar System
Depending on your own expertise and the state of your equipment, there is a variety of radio observations accessible to the amateur. Simple detection of individual sources, such as Cassiopeia A or the Crab Nebula, can be a satisfying achievement; and you can confirm that you really have found what you were looking for by taking advantage of lunar occultations. Occultations of strong radio sources are usually predicted well in advance; if you hear that one is due, set up your system and try to catch it.

It is also possible to use the distant sources to find out more about our own planet. Radio sources scintillate just as stars twinkle, and for a similar reason. The scintillation is caused by uneven transmission of radio signals through the ionosphere of the Earth, and the structure of the ionosphere is still not very well understood. In addition, there are scintillation effects produced by the tenuous interplanetary medium; it is interesting that the fascinating radio stars known as pulsars were discovered at Cambridge University during a programme which was intended to investigate scintillation.

Satellites
I'm not sure if it really counts as radio astronomy, but many people take an interest in listening to artifical satellites. Indeed, one famous group of amateurs, at Kettering Grammar School in England, has been known to scoop the professionals on more than one occasion with reports of new launchings by Soviet space scientists, or unusual behaviour of satellites after launch.

So there is plenty of scope for someone with a knowledge of radio and electronics to dabble in astronomy. This introductory outline will hardly do more than let you know that it is feasible to consider radio astronomy as a hobby—but even that might be useful news. And remember that a great deal of the ground already covered in this book in sections on optical astronomy can be translated into the basis of a radio astronomy hobby, if you have the appropriate electronic knowledge.

Where to Begin—Useful Organizations

It may seem a bit odd to find an Appendix, at the end of a book, telling you where to begin. But everything in this book is no more than a preparation for the adventure of making your own astronomical observations, and you will need more than I can provide here if you are to take a serious interest in the opportunities offered by this hobby. It would be foolish (both for me and for you) to think that anyone could get very far armed with this material alone, although I hope that by the time you have got this far you will have gained a little better understanding of the night sky, perhaps tried your hand at astronomical photography, and just possibly cadged a look through someone's telescope. And if you have got this far, it seems more than likely that you will want to move on to better things—so this is where you should begin your real astronomical hobby.

The first step is to start subscribing to the magazine *Sky and Telescope,* published by Sky Publishing Corporation, 49-50-51 Bay State Road, Cambridge, Massachusetts 02138, USA, or at least to find a library which takes the magazine. This contains a lot of material particularly relevant for the dedicated amateur or semi-professional, but it also has a lot of valuable information for the beginner. Not the least among its many assets are the advertisements for astronomical equipment, both new and secondhand, and the means it provides for getting in touch with other amateur astronomers. In the USA, there is no formally constituted national organization for astronomers who regard themselves as beginners or casual hobbyists, but there are many local societies. You may be able to find your nearest group through a local telephone directory or by asking around; however, *Sky and Telescope* publishes a special issue each year with information about local societies, so look in your local library.

Two US societies merit special mention here: the **Association of Lunar and Planetary Observers** (Box AZ, University Park, New Mexico) is an amateur organization which has a widespread reputation (although I have had no contact with it myself) and the **Astronomical Society of the Pacific** (675 Eighteenth Av, San Francisco 21, California) is an organization with both amateur and professional members, and a special interest in astronomy teaching, in the broadest sense.

Further north, the **Royal Astronomical Society of Canada** has many amateur members (although perhaps it is not an ideal organization for the complete novice) and also many branches; so if you wish to contact them try the phone book for the address of the nearest; and on the other side of the world, I am told that the **Royal Astronomical Society of New Zealand** (Carter Observatory, Wellington) also welcomes amateurs.

Indeed, the **Royal Astronomical Society** (Burlington House, Piccadilly, London W1) also has amateur members. But I would not recommend you to start by making contact with this society, since Britain is perhaps the best organized country of all for amateur astronomers at a national level.

The principal amateur organization in the UK is the **British Astronomical Association,** usually known as the BAA, which can be contacted at the Royal Astronomical Society's Burlington House address. If you progress to making a worthwhile contribution to programmes of, say, meteor watching, then it's probable, if you live in the UK, that it will be to the BAA that you make your reports about lights in the sky, and that it will be through the BAA that your observations are related to those of other amateurs for overall analysis. The BAA holds regular meetings and publishes various publications. But it is not really a happy home for the more casual astronomical hobbyist.

For the complete beginner in the UK there is the **Junior Astronomical Society,** or JAS. Don't be put off by the name, which the JAS is always planning to change but never quite does; the society is for 'junior astronomers', that is people with little or no experience, but of any age. The society publishes a quarterly magazine *Hermes* and a circular with various observational notes (and small ads for second hand telescopes and so on!). They are the ideal people to put you in touch with local societies, and (to my mind their greatest asset) members of the JAS have not lost the feeling that astronomy is fun. Perhaps for this reason, the society retains many members who can hardly be counted as junior astronomers any more, and although in theory the natural scheme of things might seem to be for the more experienced amateur to move on from the JAS to active membership of the BAA, there is only any real point in this if you wish to take your hobby as a 'serious' amateur activity.

So for the British reader the next step is simple and obvious: contact the JAS at 58 Vaughan Gardens, Ilford, Essex IG1 3PD (Secretary: V. L. Tibbott).

In other countries the choice is more restricted, but it should not prove too difficult to find the name and address of some kind of astronomical organization. If all else fails, don't hesitate to write to one of the great observatories; professional astronomers are usually happy to encourage beginners (many of them started out the same way) and will probably put you in contact with other amateurs. But please do *write,* and wait patiently for the reply. You are not likely to meet with a warm response if you turn up in the middle of the night asking for a 'look through the telescopes'. This does happen—I well remember one occasion when a colleague and I were trying to do some quiet skygazing at the Lick Observatory and were interrupted by a rather incoherent gentleman who claimed to have driven all the way from Washington DC specially to see us, and seemed more interested in the possibility of using the 120-inch to look into the windows of houses in downtown San Jose than in the wonders of the heavens! Somehow I doubt that he was a genuine seeker after astronomical knowledge; but if he was, I fear we probably put him off for life.

Further Reading

The following books are only a small selection of those available, and if you can't find any of them, you should be able to find alternatives in your library. But there is a great range in quality in astronomical books (as in most other things), as well as a broad spectrum at different technical levels, so if you find a particular book too technical or poorly written, discard it and move on to something more suited to your own needs. Just as there is no point in persevering with, say, comet studies if you are temperamentally better suited to photographing gaseous nebulae, there is no point in persevering with a book you can't get to grips with.

Basic astronomy books

Meteorites and Their Origins by G. J. McCall
Halsted Press, 1973
Fairly technical, but contains just about everything you might want to know about the subject.

Naked Eye Astronomy by Patrick Moore
Norton, 1966
Although the author cheats a bit on the title, by mentioning how to view the Sun with a telescope, no reader will mind that. A good basic guide.

Amateur Astronomy by Patrick Moore
Norton, Revised ed.
Originally entitled *The Amateur Astronomer*, 1968.

Standard Handbook for Telescope Making by N. E. Howard
T. Y. Crowell, 1959
No more technical than necessary; a good guide for the practically inclined.

Telescopes: How to Make Them, How to Use Them, Ed. by T. Page and L. W. Page
Macmillan, 1966
A series of articles originally published in *Sky and Telescope,* some very old. Readable and informative.

Radio astronomy

Radio Astronomy Simplified by John Heywood
Arco, 1963
Technical, but good if you can still find a copy.

Radio Astronomy for Amateurs by Frank Hyde
Norton, 1963
Not written in an easy style, but contains a wealth of valuable information. Do, however, ignore what the author says about the nature of celestial radio sources, which is out of date and incorrect.

Artificial Satellite Observing and Its Applications by H. Miles
American Elsevier, 1974
This is a disappointing book in some respects, and misses out on the opportunity to provide a really definitive account. But it is worth reading, and especially good in providing information about radio tracking and monitoring of satellites.

Everyman's Astronomy Ed. by R. H. Stoy
St. Martins, 1975
A valuable mini-encyclopedia. The only flaw with this book is that it contains little about the most recent developments in astronomy (discoveries made since about 1970); but that is not a serious problem for the astronomical hobbyist.

Collins Concise Encyclopedia of Astronomy
Collins, Glasgow and Follett, Chicago, 1968
Barely adequate, but very cheap.

Astrophysics

Stellar Evolution by A. J. Meadows
Pergamon, 1967
Good straightforward account of what makes stars "tick."

Index